Beverly A. Matthews
107 N. Orr, Unit A
Normal, Illinos 61761

Beverly Ann Matthews
1106 E. Washington St.
Bloomington, Illinois 61701

1917

RED BANNERS, WHITE MANTLE

WARREN H. CARROLL

CHRISTENDOM PUBLICATIONS
Crossroads Books
Route 3, Box 87
Front Royal, Virginia 22630

LC Cat. Card No.: D 639.R4C3
ISBN: 0-931888-05-0

NIHIL OBSTAT:
✠ Rev. Edward Berbusse, *Censor Deputatus*
November 2, 1981

IMPRIMATUR:
Most Rev. Thomas J. Welsh
Bishop of Arlington
November 2, 1981

CONTENTS

November 21, 1916

His Imperial and Apostolic Majesty Francis Joseph, of the House of Habsburg, was eighty-six years old. For sixty-eight years—the longest reign in European history—he had been Emperor of Austria, Apostolic King of Hungary, direct successor to the Holy Roman Emperors of old who had been the temporal heads and bulwarks of Christendom, the defenders of the faithful against infidel foes without and within. For almost half a thousand years, the Catholic empire of central Europe—the Holy Roman Empire and its immediate successor, the Empire of Austria-Hungary—had been in the hands of the Habsburg family. Now weakened, gravely threatened, it yet remained the only principle of unity for the jumbled peoples of the Balkans, the last thoroughly Catholic monarchy on earth.

Almost every day of his sixty-eight years of rule, Francis Joseph had worked on duties of state. His bed was an army camp cot. Beside it was the kneeler and stand where he asked his beloved God for the daily help that alone could have sustained him through such a life as he had led.

Long ago in that distant year of Europe-wide revolution, 1848, Francis Joseph had come to power in a torn and distracted land on the bayonets of grand old Marshal Radetzky and thin-lipped, vengeful Windischgratz. His father was feeble-minded, his termagant mother more hindrance than help. The renowned Metternich, the Austrian architect of post-Napoleonic Europe, had fled for his life, never to return. An eighteen-year-old emperor,

5

Francis Joseph stood alone. In the years of struggle that followed he put his trust in God, freed the Church in Austria from the bonds which Metternich had fastened upon her, devised the dual monarchy of Austria and Hungary, and preserved his heritage.

The years rolled on, one after another bringing hammer-blows directly upon Francis Joseph's stout heart. His brother Maximilian was shot by the Church's sworn enemies at Queretaro in Mexico, on the Hill of the Bells. His only son, Crown Prince Rudolf, shot himself and his secret lover at the hunting lodge of Mayerling. His adored wife Elizabeth, the most beautiful woman in Europe, was stabbed to death by an anarchist on the still blue shores of Lake Geneva; in her room, carefully preserved, her rosary still hung. And on June 28, 1914 his nephew and heir, the Archduke Francis Ferdinand, was shot to death with his wife in a car at Sarajevo by a Serbian killer named Princip, with the known connivance of the Serbain government. When that last appalling blow fell upon him, at the age of eighty-three, for once in the roll of iron years Francis Joseph broke down and wept, crying: "I am spared nothing!" He went to war to crush Serbia as a nest of assassins—and pulled all Europe after him into a war for the world that undermined the foundations of civilization itself.

Now it was late autumn of 1916—gray days and chill, and some of the cold crept past the fires that burned in the porcelain stoves of room after room of the Imperial and Royal Hofburg in the heart of Vienna, and splendid Schonbrunn on the outskirts, to touch the aged form of this dogged, dauntless man who was, after all, not indestructible. He fought back. He was a soldier, a Habsburg, heir of the Holy Roman Emperors; fifty million people depended on him. For ten days the sweat and chills of fever came and went. He never stopped working. But his court chamberlain summoned a young man of twenty-nine to hurry from his duties in the field to Vienna "in view of the condition of the Emperor." For this young man with an open face and a boyish smile, whose name was Charles, had become heir to Francis Joseph, to his mighty office and heritage and his overwhelming responsibilites, when the crime of Sarajevo launched the First World War.

Charles came. He greeted his wife of five years—dark-eyed,

vivacious, highly intelligent Zita—and their little son Otto, four years old. Charles and Zita went to see the old Emperor. It was November 21, 1916, about eleven o'clock in the morning.

When Francis Joseph heard that they were coming, he asked them to wait until he had changed into his military jacket which he always wore when receiving visitors. A lifetime's habits of formality were not easily set aside, but Zita insisted that he not make the effort, and he gave way. They talked only a little while. The Emperor spoke of good news from the military front, but especially of how happy he was to have recently received the special blessing of the Pope. He was still in command of himself and of his realm, as he had been all through those sixty-eight years of the loneliness of command.

In the short November afternoon, Francis Joseph felt a great weakness coming upon him. He understood what it meant. He knew he faced death, and he knew death faced his empire, hard beset by the enormous, incalculable perils of a world disintegrating under the stresses of a conflict far more protracted and cosmically destructive than anyone had imagined possible. And he knew the quality of the radiant young couple who had visited with him that morning: their goodness, their hope, their relative innocence, their inexperience, their crystal simplicity of purpose and conviction, but with scarcely a trace of the touch of the ruthless which is very close to being necessary in a temporal ruler in this fallen world.

As the afternooon wore on and twilight fell over Vienna, he said:

> I took over the throne under the most difficult conditions and I am leaving it under even worse ones. I would like to have spared Charles this. But he is made of the right stuff, and will know how to cope.(1)

These are among the last recorded words of Emperor Francis Joseph. When Charles and Zita returned, about seven o'clock that evening, he was already in a coma. At five minutes past nine he died.

War Upon The World, 1914-1916

For twenty-eight terrible months the guns had thundered, unavailing. Europe, the fountainhead of Western civilization, the capital of the world, ran red with blood. The bare casualty statistics alone touch the unimaginable: in the first three weeks of the war, more than a million men; in the year 1915, more than four million; in 1916, two and a quarter million on the Western front alone.

These gigantic losses were not suffered in a struggle for some overriding moral or religious principle or right that might not be sacrificed at any cost. Except for one small country, Belgium, the war did not involve any nation's essential freedom or existence. It was a war of fronts in border regions, a war of trenches and attrition, a war that pitted the deadly machine gun against unprotected human flesh. A million men bled or died during ten months before Verdun, from February to October, 1916; when the ghastly grapple ended, both French and Germans held exactly the positions they had held when it started. On the Somme, in the summer of 1916, over six hundred thousand British and French soldiers were killed or wounded to gain just eight miles, and 650,000 Germans were killed or wounded to limit them to that. Those eight miles cost the life or health of thirty men for every foot, two and a half men for every inch. On one single day at the Somme—July 1, 1916—the British army lost sixty thousand men, one-third of them killed, the largest single day's loss of men in the thousand-year history of the British army.

It had begun at Sarajevo; where it would end, no man could guess. Only scattered, unheeded voices spoke for peace: Pope Benedict XV, "the little fellow," frail, intense, supremely dedicated, pleading and praying from Rome for an end to the orgy of killing that was destroying much of what remained of Christendom, but almost totally ignored by Catholic as well as by Protestant nations; Woodrow Wilson, President of the United States, offering a mediation that nobody wanted, which was too distantly based to do any real good; and a handful of Marxist revolutionaries, who saw that the war would destroy much of the moral and material fabric of the Christian civilization that presented the most fundamental obstacle to their seizure of power, and were jockeying for position to pick up the pieces. Nationalist passions had risen to absurd, almost incredible heights. Englishmen, Frenchmen, and Russians with German names were often in actual physical danger; on both sides, with a demented tenacity, virtually every significant national leader continued to demand total victory, whatever the price, even though no victories of real significance had been won by either side since the first month of the war, that fateful August of 1914.

Each side, then had been sure it could win. There were two great alliances: the Entente (France, Great Britain, Russia) and the Central Powers (Germany, Austria-Hungary, Turkey). Each was bound together by a tight network of treaties—some public, some secret. Russia was allied with Serbia, then the leading Slav state in the Balkans. When Austria issued a fiercely inflexible ultimatum to Serbia after the assassination of Archduke and imperial heir Francis Ferdinand by the killers the Serbian government had aided—an ultimatum whose acceptance would require a virtual Austrian takeover of the country—Russia felt bound to come to Serbia's aid. When, a month after the assassination, Austria declared war on Serbia after Serbia had rejected the ultimatum, the Russian government faced a grim dilemma: the vastness of their country, the largest in the world, and the relatively poor condition of their transportation system meant that a general mobilization would take substantially longer in Russia than anywhere else. To wait for the other powers to mobilize was to court defeat. Therefore, after two days of agonized vacillation, Czar Nicholas ordered Russian mobilization, even though he knew it meant world war. All the other five great powers

in the two alliances followed suit within hours; and the Russian
mobilization immediately triggered Germany's Schlieffen Plan.

Von Schlieffen, former chief of the German Imperial General
Staff, now lay in his grave; but his strategy had become the basis
of all German military planning for a general European war: strike
Belgium without warning, outflanking through Belgian territory
the mighty French defenses on the Alsatian frontier; keeping the
right wing strong, make a vast turning movement to envelop Paris
and knock France out of the war; then defeat in detail the
numerous but much less well equipped Russian armies, leaving
Germany the strongest power on the European continent, with
which Great Britain for all its dominant sea power would then have
to come to terms.

It was a brilliant plan, one of the most brilliant in military
history. But it overlooked two vital factors, one moral, one
material. The moral factor—the only real moral issue of this war,
other than the relatively limited evil of the Sarajevo assassination
itself—was the magnitude of the crime it required to be
committed: the sudden descent of millions of German soldiers
upon a small free country, Belgium, that had done no harm to
anyone and threatened no one, occupying it ruthlessly,
obliterating some of its national treasures, conscripting its citizens
into an alien and hated war effort, without a trace of rational or
moral justification that even the cleverest German apologist could
think of, except for the military imperatives of the Schlieffen Plan
itself. The material factor, unnoticed by almost all the world's
generals and planners, was that for once in the history of war the
strength of defensive weaponry far exceeded that of the offensive.
For the machine gun had arrived, while the tank still tarried. The
machine gun ruled any fixed battlefield. There was no answer to it,
no defense against it. Even a few days' stabilization of the
battle-front, enough to permit machine guns to be emplaced in a
protective trench system, would make that front for all practical
purposes impregnable.

In August 1914, the one and only month of the war when free
maneuver was possible on the Western front, the German armies
routed the Russians at Tannenberg and the Masurian Lakes in

East Prussia, but were stopped before Paris, at the Marne, by a brilliant counter-stroke by one of the only two really able generals the Entente powers produced in the whole war: Gallieni of France. (The other, Marshal Foch, held no major command until 1918.) By the end of 1914, on the Western front, the trench lines ran, bristling with machine guns, from Switzerland to the English Channel. In the east, the situation did not fully stabilize in this manner until the end of 1915, with all of Poland in German or Austrian hands and the Russians driven out of it: after that, there was hardly any more movement on the Eastern front than on the Western—only the endless, dreadful, unremitting slaughter.

One imaginative attempt was made in 1915 to break the iron ring: the attack on Gallipoli, Winston Churchill's project, intended to break through the straits controlled by Turkey of the Central Powers to open a direct route of supply and support to the Black Sea ports of hard-pressed Russia. Ineptly conducted by wooden-headed, clay-footed commanders afloat and ashore, the Gallipoli offensive of the mistress of the seas and many of the finest soldiers of the British Empire was brought to a grinding halt in a few days chiefly by the exertions of a young Turkish commander named Mustapha, later to take the name of Kemal Ataturk. The trenches were run, the machine guns took over, the Entente lost a quarter of a million men and never gained more than a square mile or two of barren, rocky Turkish coast.

By the end of 1915 if not by the end of 1914, it should have been obvious to every statesman and general in Europe that no man or nation could win this war and that the whole of Western civilization was losing it. The extension of the war through 1916, and then on through 1917 and most of 1918, was an act of mad folly unsurpassed, and scarcely paralleled, in the whole history of mankind in magnitude and shattering consequences. Yet not a single statesman or general in any of the warring powers spoke out for any peace short of victory for his side. And *all* allies had to be satisfied; any one of them could block peace, and by the perverted moral code of the alliances, their veto must be respected. The very word "peace" was all but forgotten, all but forbidden; to speak it, even to think it, was "defeatism" and close to treason.

All the resources, human and material, of the warring powers
were flung unrestrainedly, unhesitatingly, as fast as they could be
thrown, into the bottomless pit of the war, the desperate struggles
for a few thousand yards here and there of blood-soaked,
shell-pocked earth. The richer nations, with more material
resources to throw, became exhausted more slowly than their
poorer allies; many were the ice-cold calculations of which
contenders would emerge with a tiny fraction of their fighting men
and national wealth intact, after the others had become totally
destitute. In England, in France, and in Germany the strain was
enormous, but for the moment, at the end of 1916, still bearable.
France, with substantial tracts of her national territory (though
still only a relatively small part of the whole) occupied by the
Germans, bore the brunt of the conflict on the Western front,
supplied a sizeable majority of the Entente troops there engaged,
and suffered a correspondingly large proportion of the losses. The
fact that French lands were occupied by an invading enemy,
together with the long-standing grievance over the German
absorption of German-speaking but traditionally French Alsace
after the Franco-Prussian War of 1870, blinded all French leaders
by nationalistic passion to the reality of their situation. Raymond
Poincare, the fierce-eyed, spade-bearded president of France, was
an uncompromisnig nationalist who hated everything German. His
prime minister, Aristide Briand, was a somewhat more reasonable
man; but reason did not hold sway in the Europe of 1916. Briand,
with Poincare, demanded victory or death.

In England the evil of the invasion and devastation of Belgium
was especially keenly felt, for Belgium was England's traditional
ward, almost a protectorate; for more than three hundred years it
had been a cardinal principle of English foreign policy not to let
Belgium, particularly its coastline, fall into the hands of a major
continental power and actual or potential enemy of England. Now
the Germans stood on the Belgian coast, at Ostend and
Zeebrugge, occupying the entire country except for a tiny sliver
around smashed Ypres near the French border and the Channel.
Ostend and Zeebrugge were just two or three hours' journey
across the narrow seas from England. The German government

had made it very clear that it would not give up its Belgian conquests, or at least not all of them; the British insisted they must all be given up, whatever the cost. Yet Great Britian, the richest country in the world, the world's banker, on whose empire the sun never set, was stretched to the limit by the gigantic struggle. Much of its food had to be imported in ships constantly menaced by German submarines. Fighting men and munitions were in dangerously short supply. In December 1916 the colorless and increasingly ineffective British Prime Minister Asquith fell; his successor was David Lloyd George, the "Welsh wizard," who had gained a great reputation both for his parliamentary skill and for the way he had overcome the worst of the munitions crisis.

Unfortunately he inherited as his supreme army commanders two generals with reputations as undeserved as they were great. Their record of sheer blind stubborn incompetence, still glossed over by many historians, is perhaps the most appalling chapter in the world's military history. Worst of all, their particular incompetence was not of the kind that would lead to their obvious defeat and therefore likely removal from command; what it did was to prevent them from either winning, or knowing when to stop their attack. They were Douglas Haig, the field commander, and William Robertson, the Chief of Staff. Lloyd George, in later, embittered retirement, after years of reflection on the disaster they had done so much to bring upon him, upon Great Britain, and upon the whole world, had this to say of them and their like:

> The tale of these battles constitutes a trilogy illustrating the unquenchable heroism that will never accept defeat and the inexhaustible vanity that will never admit a mistake. It is the story of the million who would rather die than own themselves cowards—even to themselves—and also of the two or three individuals who would rather the million perish than that they as leaders should own—even to themselves—that they were blunderers. Hence the immortal renown and the ghastly notoriety of the Verdun, Somme and Passchendaele battlefields; the fame won by sustained valour unrivalled in the annals of war; the notoriety attained by a narrow and stubborn egotism, unsurpassed amongst the records of disaster wrought by human complacency.(2)

His searing verdict has been called spiteful, personally exculpatory, overstated. Whatever may have been his own responsiblity for the Passchendaele campaign, so far as these words relate to the generals in overall command of these battles, they are no more than just.

Germany was still immensely strong, though obviously she could not endure the strain forever. While France and Great Britain were determined to win back what had been lost in France and Belgium, Germany was equally determined to hold on at least to most of it, and to her gains in the east, convinced that she was so far the victor. This was, unquestioningly and uncompromisingly, the attitude of the oddly assorted duo who by 1916 had come to be in effective charge of the whole German war effort: General Paul von Hindenburg, *der alte Kerl*, "the old fellow," in looks and mien and speech the very image of what Germans most admired in their military tradition, but of limited intelligence and imagination; and Erich von Ludendorff, young, abrasive, brilliant—and pitiless, a man who always believed that the end justified the means. But Germany still had civilian government, under Chancellor Theobald von Bethmann-Hollweg, who had retained considerable influence with Kaiser Wilhelm II, his old friend. Bethmann-Hollweg's honesty and integrity are apparent from his extraordinary public admission, in the earliest days of the war, that the German invasion of Belgium had been morally unjustified, though he nevertheless excused it on grounds of military necessity, and promised to try to make it up to Belgium after the war. Though Bethmann-Hollweg did not quite have the moral courage to seek peace openly—and would certainly have lost office almost immediately if he had—at least he tried to keep doors open to the possibility of peace, and consistently opposed further widening of the war, as by bringing the United States in by launching the German submarines against all neutral ships in British waters.

For imperial Austria and imperial Russia, the situation by November 1916 was not only increasingly perilous and eventually intolerable; it was already on the brink of total and final disaster. Neither state was as strong or as wealthy as Great Britain, France or Germany. The Austro-Hungarian Empire was a collection of some twenty nationalities and tongues, with a great and ancient heritage of unity through the persons of the Habsburg rulers, but increasingly divided as modern nationalistic agitation worked on its diverse peoples. Emperor Francis Joseph, for all his devoted and ceaseless efforts, had not been able to maintain the fullness of supervision and control at eighty-four and eighty-five and eighty-six that a younger man could have provided; and he had, as ever, very little help. Russian manpower outnumbered Austrian by three to one. Between their support services, their national economies, and their generalship there was little to choose. Numbers alone would have beaten Austria had Germany not been her ally; even with German help, necessarily limited because of Germany's enormous commitment on the Western front, the stress was steadily wearing Austria down toward the point where the delicate intertwining structure of the "multinational empire" would suddenly unravel into all its twenty-odd components.

The Emperor was the symbol of unity. Only in the Emperor, in the house of Habsburg, was there hope for the continuity of the Austro-Hungarian regime. Young Charles now incarnated that hope, and bore it well.

In Russia also, the Czar was the symbol of unity, not only of the diverse peoples of his vast land, but of the Russian people themselves. But he was more than a symbol. Like Louis XIV, and unlike Charles, the Czar *was* the state. There was a considerable degree of local self-government in the Austrian empire, virtually none at all in the Russian empire. The Czar was truly, as his title declared, Autocrat of all the Russias. So it had been at least since Ivan the Terrible, if not since Genghis Khan.

But there was this fundamental difference between the regime of Czar Nicholas II and that of his grim predecessors: Genghis Khan was no Christian, and Ivan the Terrible a very bad one. Although two later famous rulers of Russia were also very indifferent Christians—Peter the Great and Catherine the Great—all the Czars since the beginning of the nineteenth century, beginning with Alexander I who defeated Napoleon, had been profoundly religious men, reflecting the deep faith of Holy Mother Russia and the simplest of its people. In a crisis of the

magnitude of this colossal war, Russia and Austria had spiritual
resources upon which to draw which, even if only in enhancing
their endurance, should have made up for their relative lack of
visible human and material resources, and eventually impelled
them more and more toward the peace of which the warring
peoples dreamed, but dared not speak.

In Austria under Charles, this is precisely what happened. But
in Russia the well was being poisoned.

* * * * *

Czar Nicholas II was a charming, gentle man, devout,
well-intentioned. But he was never master in his own house, where
his wife Alexandra ruled, and only rarely and briefly master of his
empire. Others ruled in his name. In the early years of his reign it
was Sergius Witte, the brilliant, caustic expert in planning and
economic development, the man primarily responsible for one of
the greatest and most historically significant engineering feats of
all time, the building of the Trans-Siberian Railroad, longest in
the world. Without his work and his legacy, Russia would hardly
have been able to sustain the burden of world war for one year, let
alone three.

Yet Russia had lost its war with Japan in 1905, though Witte's
skill in negotiation had wrung surprisingly favorable terms from
the Oriental victors, and the defeat had been followed by an
attempt at revolution. To help gather the support necessary to
suppress the rising, Czar Nicholas was forced to agree to share
some of his power with an elected parliament, the Duma, the first
body of its kind in Russian history. Perversely, he blamed Witte
for this, since Witte had long recommended such action, and never
again trusted him with any public office.

Then came Peter Stolypin, no genius, but a competent and
discerning man who clearly saw that the Russian peasant, long a
serf, still largely dwelling in communal farms in which he had little
personal stake, should be aided in every possible way to obtain
enough land to support himself and his family, thereby giving him
solid economic and personal reasons to sustain the state. The

"kulaks," landowning private farmers, whom the Communists were later to liquidate by the millions, were essentially the creation of Peter Stolypin. But in 1911 Stolypin was murdered by a renegade policeman. The motives of the assassin, whether he was involved in conspiracy and if so for what purpose, have never been established.

There was a man who had prophesied Stolypin's death, saying, as he drove his carriage through the streets behind the Czar and Czarina the day before his assassination: "Death is after him! Death is driving behind him!"(3) This man came from Siberia, from the village of Pokrovskoe in the province of Tobolsk, 250 miles beyond the Ural mountains, amid endless leagues of dark forests where, in winter, the temperature drops to forty degrees below zero. His father Efim was a horse thief; his name was Gregory, and early in his adult life his sexual promiscuity and prowess gained him the surname Rasputin, the Dissolute, which ever afterward he used. There were rumors of his connection with the *khlysti*, whose rites, like the pagan "mysteries" of ancient Greece and Rome, combined sexual orgies—including sadism, masochism, and promiscuous intercourse—with fervid expressions of devotion to superhuman beings who were involved in some way in the orgies. Bishop Antony of Tobolsk had denounced Rasputin, who had then disappeared into the Siberian forests. He roamed over much of the immensity of Russia, proclaiming his conversion to a holy and mystical Christian life; he went twice to Jerusalem, and once to the most famous monastery of all the Eastern Orthodox Church, at Mount Athos in Greece. In 1903 he had appeared at the Orthodox Christian academy in St. Petersburg, introducing himself as a wandering monk, a *starets*—a way of life and a calling hallowed by centuries of Russian Christian tradition. He was received by the famous Father John of Kronstadt, and accepted as a holy man. Departing for a time, he returned to St. Petersburg in 1905, the year of abortive revolution. Then he met Archimandrite Theophan, Inspector of the Theological Academy in St. Petersburg, who had been the Empress Alexandra's confessor, and Bishop Hermogen of Saratov. Both were favorably impressed by this man who seemed to them well fitted to be a strong and articulate link with the peasants of Russia and their profound, enduring faith.

Evidently these three genuine men of God—Father John of Kronstadt, Archimandrite Theophan, and Bishop Hermogen—had not received the gift of the discernment of spirits.

Alongside Russian Orthodox faith and practice, there had spread among the high society of the Russian capital at this period a dangerous fascination with the occult. Seances were much in vogue. Tales of clairvoyants and poltergeists were breathlessly exchanged. Two princesses from the tiny Balkan Slavic country of Montenegro, Militsa and Anastasia, were leaders in these chic spiritualistic activities. It was Militsa who first introduced Rasputin to the Czar and his family, in November of 1905, when revolutionary activity of that year in Russia was just passing its peak. He had already gained a great reputation as a healer; and the heir to all the Russias stood in need of healing which no earthly power or knowledge could give.

The first four children of Nicholas and Alexandra had all been girls. Since Czar Paul had changed the law of imperial succession at the end of the eighteenth century out of hatred for the memory of his overpowering mother, Catherine the Great, royal succession in Russia had passed only through the male line, to males. Therefore, if Nicholas and Alexandra had no sons, Nicholas' oldest brother or his sons would provide the heir. Alexandra, who loved her husband and children profoundly and passionately, but had always felt estranged from his relatives, wanted above all else to give Nicholas an heir. At last, in 1904, a son was born to them, and named Alexis. There were no more children.

But is was soon discovered that Alexis had hemophilia, that still incurable deficiency in the clotting element in the blood, passed from generation to generation through a recessive gene linked to the male chromosome, so that it is found exclusively in boys and men, though the gene is carried by their mothers. In the hemophiliac, the stream of blood which every man holds within his body may break loose at any moment, causing agonizing pain and threatening life itself. The great danger is internal bleeding, from the nose or mouth, or especially from any bruise. In the hemophiliac, the bleeding which makes a bruise may continue for days instead of the normal few minutes, causing terrible pain from the pressure of the accumulated blood. Special stress on the joints may cause prolonged bleeding into them. Any injury even moderately severe meant, in those days, almost sure death for the sufferer from hemophilia.

The nature of Alexis' affliction was kept secret from almost all of Russia, in the fear that it would undermine the throne itself. Alexandra, who suffered terribly under the constant threat to her adored son and the necessity of watching helplessly as he endured for hours and days the intense pain resulting from each episode of internal bleeding, prayed with all the ardor of her naturally ardent soul for a miraculous cure. None was forthcoming. Instead, Rasputin came.

He was a man of unforgettable appearance. Even in still black and white, his photograph may send a sharp thrill of unease through the reader, as the shocking image seems almost to jump from the page. His hair and beard were long and coal-black, often matted and tangled and encrusted with dirt. He rarely washed or changed his clothes. His nose was broad and fleshy and his lips were full. But his most striking features were his hands and his eyes. His hands were long and large, with thick fingers, and almost constantly moving—not in quick, gesticulating motions, but rhythmically, caressingly. His eyes were an almost colorless blue-gray, large and steady, sometimes brilliant, sometimes seeming to contract almost to pinpoints. Using hands and eyes together, he could hypnotize in a very short time anyone willing to submit himself to him—and even some initially without that intention. He once tried to hypnotize Stolypin, a good man of strong will and bluff common sense, who resisted him firmly and successfully; but even he, despite his overwhelming loathing, felt the power of those hands and eyes.

It soon became unmistakably clear, not only to the distressed and desperate Alexandra, but to everyone in her household, that Rasputin could stop Alexis' bleeding and ease his pain. It is possible to explain many—though not all—of these healings by natural or hypnotic suggestion, which some controlled medical experiments have shown to be of value in treating hemophilia by bringing down blood pressure and checking the flow of blood to the smaller vessels through a relaxation emanating from the autonomic nervous system. But some instances of the healing of Alexis were from a distance, and these no such theory can explain—notably the healing by a telegraph message, when Alexis was at the point of death from a massive internal hemorrhage in the leg brought on by a fall on an oarlock in a boat, while the royal family was staying at the Polish hunting lodge of Spala in 1912.

Seeing in Rasputin, the "man of God," the answer to her prayers in a sure protection for her son from agony and death, Alexandra drew him into the bosom of her family and lavished upon him all the ardent, outpouring gratitude and love of her whole-hearted personality, so rarely displayed in public. She would hear no evil of him and see no evil in him. Against the fervent totality of her endorsement Czar Nicholas had no defense. It is likely that from time to time he doubted Rasputin; but he never found the strength of will to prevail in any matter connected with the one whom Alexandra always called "our Friend."

By 1911, the year Stolypin was assassinated after Rasputin had predicted his imminent death, Rasputin was known as a very important figure at court. Emphasizing to all his influence and intimacy with the royal family, he passed on the most gushing and indiscreet remarks of Nicholas and Alexandra in his praise, such as Nicholas telling him "you are Christ,"(4) and Alexandra writing him: "I kiss your hands and lean my head on your blessed shoulder. Oh how light, how light do I feel then. I only wish one thing: to fall asleep, to fall asleep forever on your shoulders and in your arms."(5) To the royal family Rasputin turned his mask of counterfeit holiness; to all others he turned the savage, leering countenance of a satyr. His shameless seduction of women—including some of the highest in the land—was notorious, exceedingly frequent, and often wide open in public. His drunkenness was as pervasive as his filth, and usually in public. Obscenities spewed from his mouth, and as he uttered them, he told his listeners that this was how he talked to the Empress of Russia.

That was a lie. But who, facing Rasputin, could be sure of the truth?

The Church in Russia is ancient, hallowed and rooted in the people and the soil. It has produced mystics, saints, and martyrs all through the near-millennium since King St. Vladimir first accepted Christ at Kiev in the year 987. Its separation from the Roman Catholic Church was, at the beginning, more historical accident than conscious schism: the Russian church, far from Rome and having almost no contact with it while having been evangelized from Constantinople, followed the Greek city and its patriarchs and missionaries without being fully aware of the countervailing claims of the successors of Peter upon their religious allegiance. But the result, as the centuries passed and Constantinople fell to the Muslim Turks in 1453, had been that Moscow came to see itself as the "third Rome," with its church indissolubly bound to its state, without any clear and generally recognized source of authority in the Church distinct from the state. Bishops and metropolitans could and did denounce religious charlatans and heretics. But the authority of the Czar, Autocrat of all the Russias, was supreme in the Russian church as in everything else that was in Russia, and could override any episcopal decree and countermand any episcopal action.

By 1911 Archimandrite Theophan, one of Rasputin's original sponsors, had heard enough of Rasputin's doings in the confessions of his aristocratic women penitents to realize much of the true nature of the man he had once recommended to the royal family. He told Alexandra to beware of him, whereupon he was immediately removed to the Crimea. Rasputin boasted: "I have shut his trap."(6) Antony, Metropolitan of St. Petersburg, came to Nicholas to warn him that the public scandal Rasputin's behavior and connection with the royal family was creating could threaten the very foundations of the Russian state, dependent as it was was the Czar and his family as the symbol of unity and trust sealed by the Faith. Nicholas told Metropolitan Antony that this was a private affair of the royal family in which he should not meddle, and dismissed him. A few months later he died.

Theophan was a gentle mystic, Antony an old and sick man;

but another of Rasputin's original sponsors, Bishop Hermogen of Saratov, was a fighter. Appalled by all that he was learning about the pretended monk from Siberia—particularly the well-authenticated report that he had recently raped a nun—Bishop Hermogen called Rasputin to his room in 1911 to confront him directly with the charges, flanked by a number of other churchmen including the popular preacher Illiodor, who for a time had been close to Rasputin and had brought many of the facts about what he had been doing to light. The imposing group cowed Rasputin, for once; he admitted the rape of the nun and other grave sexual sins. But he showed no contrition, only fear, and Bishop Hermogen was suddenly overcome by the almost irresistible urge felt and described by many good men when they came in close contact with Rasputin—the urge to attack him physically, to make a sudden maximum effort to destroy a monstrous presence. (Grand Duke Nicholas, the Czar's cousin and Russia's ablest general in the world war, a strong and high-minded man, once heard from Rasputin that he planned a visit to the front where Nicholas commanded, to bless an icon. "Yes, do come," replied the outspoken "Nikolasha," "I'll hang you." (7) Michael Rodzyanko, president of the Duma, once threw Rasputin out of the Cathedral of Our Lady of Kazan by the scruff of the neck.) Shouting, "You are smashing our sacred vessels," Bishop Hermogen struck Rasputin in the face with his fist and beat his head with a heavy cross. He and the others then made him swear on an icon henceforth to stay away from women and from the Czar's family. Later Rasputin asked Bishop Hermogen to forgive him. But the Bishop did not believe in his sincerity. Perhaps he felt that there was a force in this man incapable of repentance. He replied shortly: "Never and nowhere."(8)

It was not at all like Christ facing a sinner. But it was a little like Christ driving out a demon.

Rasputin went to the Empress with his doctored version of what had happened in Bishop Hermogen's rooms. Within a few weeks Hermogen was deprived of his ecclesiastical office and shut up in a monastery. Illiodor was imprisoned, forbidden to exercise his priesthood, and forced out of the country.

The war came. Rasputin always claimed he had opposed the war. Certainly its genesis and horrors owed nothing to him. But he took full advantage of it to enhance his position. After the Russian defeats in the summer of 1915 had required withdrawal from the whole of Poland, the Czar relieved Grand Duke Nicholas of command and, against the unanimous advice of his ministers and best supporters, went to army headquarters himself to take personal command, leaving the government in Petrograd in the hands of Alexandra—which now meant in the hands of Rasputin. The decision to remove Grand Duke Nicholas, though triggered by the military setbacks he had suffered, was ultimately due to pressure from the Empress, since she well knew his attitude toward Rasputin. From this point on, every minister in the government of Russia held office only on Rasputin's sufferance; as they were dropped, their replacements were mostly chosen directly or indirectly by Rasputin. All Russia knew it, just as all Russia knew the despicable story of Rasputin at the Yar restaurant in Moscow on April 8, 1915, where at one of the most notorious of the city's low-life haunts he had exposed himself and announced to all present that he was in the habit of doing exactly that in front of the royal family. The police had presented the Czar with a full, circumstantial report of the Yar incident; he had done nothing.

By February 1916 Rasputin had placed his creature, the petty, corrupt schemer Sturmer, as prime minister, replacing the aged and incompetent, but at least honest and sane Goremykin. The Sturmer appointment was violently unpopular, not just because of the appointee's German name—though that certainly did not help—but because of his dishonesty and his total lack of any perceptible qualifications. Shulgin, an intelligent and loyal supporter of the Czar, described him as "absolutely unprincipled and a complete nullity."(9) Foreign Minister Sazonov, the ablest man remaining in the cabinet, said Sturmer was "a man who had left a bad memory wherever he had occupied an administrative post."(10)

Sturmer at first held not only the prime ministerial office, but the post of Minister of the Interior as well, one of the most important in the government, responsible for internal security and for allocating Russia's dwindling food supplies. His sole concern seemed to be maintaining himself in office. The Director of Police during much of 1916, Klimovich, later stated that in six months he spoke with Sturmer for a total of no more than five hours, half of which time "was taken up with the affairs of Rasputin." Eventually the Ministry of the Interior was given to the absurd, half-mad Protopopov, "pretty Polly," who was highly recommended by Rasputin. Gradually Rasputin and Sturmer forced out the able, more honest and more independent ministers. Grand Duke Nicholas, former commander of the army, and Director of Police Klimovich both described Sturmer's government during 1916 as virtual chaos. A veritable parade of warnings, in writing and in person, impassioned and desperate, pleading and hoping against hope, came to Czar Nicholas from his closest relatives and truest friends, as well as from Russian patriots of every class and position who had some inkling of what was happening. Some of these appeals he dismissed in rare flashes of uncharacteristic petulance; more he gently parried; the most hard-driven and convincing he seemed to respond to, only to retreat again when a confrontation loomed with Alexandra, and the shadow of Rasputin behind her.

In November 1916 Nicholas at last nerved himself for a real decision. Rasputin had now transferred his support from Sturmer, whose trouble-making potential he had wrung dry, to Protopopov; Sturmer was dismissed. The senior remaining minister, Trepov of Transport, was asked by the Czar to form a caretaker government. An opponent of Rasputin, one of the last left among the ministers, Trepov refused unless Protopopov were removed as Minister of the Interior. Nicholas decided to remove Protopopov, explicitly telling Alexandra in a letter November 10: "I beg, do not drag Our Friend into this. The responsibility is with me, and therefore I wish to be free in my choice."(11)

As soon as she read this, Alexandra unleashed every weapon she had to break the will of the man she loved. It is hard to believe that in doing so she was acting entirely, or primarily, on her own volition.

Tell me you are not angry with me. They [Protopopov and Sturmer] bow before His [Rasputin's—capitalization in the original] wisdom. . . . All my trust is in Our Friend, who only thinks of you, Baby [Alexis] and Russia, and guided by him we shall get through this heavy time. It will be a hard fight, but a Man of God is near to guard you safely through the reefs, and little Sunny [herself] is standing as a rock behind you, firm and unwavering with decision, faith and love to fight for her darlings and our country. . . . Don't go and change Protopopov now . . . Don't change anyone until we meet, I entreat you . . . Quieten me, promise, forgive. It is for you and Baby I fight. . . . I am but a woman fighting for her master and her child . . . Only don't pull the sticks away on which I have found it possible to rest . . . You were alone with us two [herself and Rasputin] against everybody.(12)

She followed up these amazing letters (the above includes extracts from several of them, written on successive days) with a visit to Nicholas at army headquarters on November 27. Her personal presence tipped the balance. He changed his mind and agreed to retain Protopopov, while ordering Trepov to remain despite his proffered resignation. Alexandra kept up the pressure, now seeking to eliminate Trepov:

I shall stand against them [Trepov and Rodzyanko, president of the Duma] with God's holy man . . . He has kept you where you are . . . Only believe more in Our Friend . . . We must give a strong country to Baby, and dare not be weak for his sake . . . draw the reins in tightly which you let loose . . . Take no big steps without warning me . . . Russia loves to feel the whip . . . How I wish I could pour my will into your veins . . . Listen to me, which means Our Friend. I suffer over you as a tender, soft-hearted child. Pardon, believe, and understand.(13)

On December 16, 1916, she received this reply from the man she had broken, her beloved husband who was responsible for the fate of one hundred and fifty million people in the midst of the most destructive war in history:

Tender thanks for the severe written scolding. I read it with a smile, because you speak to me as though I was a child . . . Your poor little weak-willed hubby.(14)

* * * * *

One hundred and twenty-seven years before 1916 the great revolution had begun in France, the revolution that has convulsed and transformed the history of the world ever since. The tidal struggles for and against the revolution and its consequences had ebbed and flowed across all Europe during that century and a quarter. But the raw naked essence of the revolutionary heritage, found in those who would cheerfully repeat and extend Robespierre's Reign of Terror, to whom the death-dealers of the Paris Commune were holy martyrs, was a fire tended only by a few. The world had been profoundly and unforgettably warned against this kind of revolution by those shattering, oft-retold events in France. Only military disasters of enormous magnitude, engendering the breakdown of civilized order and of a functioning economy—as had happened in Paris under German siege and following the French defeat in the Franco-Prussian War of 1870-71, leading to the horrors of the Commune—held out any realistic prospect of bringing the revolution to power in any major nation.

The revolutionaries considered themselves makers of history, yet were often swept along by its currents. Almost all of them succumbed to the tremendous outburst of nationalistic emotion with which the First World War began. The Second Socialist (Marxist) International had collapsed in 1914 because virtually no international feeling remained among its members. Georgi Plekhanov, the famous Russian revolutionary Socialist leader exiled to Switzerland, said he would welcome victory by the Entente; Karl Kautsky, the equally famous German revolutionary Socialist leader, said the same about his Central Powers.

One revolutionary leader stood apart, breasting the tide, immune to passing enthusiasms, untouched by nationalism, impossible to divert from the ultimate objective. His fellow Socialists, he said, had revealed "rotten, base and mean opportunism" by supporting the war, "thereby giving a splendid impetus to the cleansing of the working-class movement from the dung accumulated during decades of peace."(15) From its outbreak until its end, through gigantic upheavals in his personal life and in the history of his cause, he denounced the war, always aware that it *could* present—for a long time he was not quite sure that it *would* present—the greatest historic opportunity for the triumph of the revolution. He was a man of coruscating political genius, above all of diamond-hard unbreakable will—the kind of man who moves mountains, if he has faith, or plumbs the depths of the abyss, if he has it not.

His name was Vladimir Ilyich Ulyanov and he came from Simbirsk on the Volga, in the very heart of Russia. He had many pen names, many aliases. The best known of them is Lenin.

Ever since his adored brother Alexander had been executed for joining in a plot to assassinate Czar Alexander III, Nicholas' father, Vladimir Ulyanov had been consumed by one fixed, yet closely reasoned purpose: to make a revolution in Russia, to overthrow the Czar and his regime as the French revolutionaries had overthrown Louis XVI and his *ancien regime*, but this time in the name of the working class, the Marxian proletariat, under the dictatorship of the party which he would build and lead, which would go on to revolutionize and conquer the world. For seventeen years he had devoted himself unremittingly to this end—in study, writing, speaking, conspiracy, organization, and an iron leadership. Lenin was not a monster. He had a happy childhood, his parents taught him Christian morality (though he rejected it), he loved music and the countryside; he could even care genuinely for people when they did not get in his way. But over and through and above all else throbbed the pounding power of his relentless will, fixed immovably on the revolution, to be achieved by any means, at any cost. His words were bullets. The most distinctive feature of his personal appearance, his big bald head, was like a bullet. Sometimes it seemed he had a bullet for a heart.

If ever one man, alone, in essence made a world-historic revolution, that man was Lenin.

By his unsparing perseverance during the years before the war, Lenin had gathered the support of a tenuous, narrow majority at Social Democratic party congresses, so that he could get away with calling his personal faction the Bolshevik Party, which means the party of the majority. But it was a majority only of a very small group—after the war began and the Second International collapsed, of a bare handful. Few paid much attention to the obscure Russian and his perfervid declarations, publications, analyses and grandiose plans which kept streaming incongruously out of Switzerland where he had gone to live, an island of complete peace in the midst of world-wracking war.

No place in all the West was quite so antithetical to everything connected with revolution as neutral Switzerland in World War I. In every sense of the phrase, Lenin was cut off. Without the help of his ever-faithful, ever-forgiving wife Nadezhda Krupskaya, tireless not only in tending him but in serving his cause even in the most menial ways—now prematurely aged and often ill, yet a tower of feminine strength to him—he might not have psychologically survived the strain and frustration. All through 1916 Lenin and Krupskaya lived in Zurich. Lenin went almost every day to the quiet, decorous, well-stocked Zurich library, dreaming amid its orderly stillness of power seized by violence in the streets of Petrograd and Moscow. But he had no way to get to either, almost no money, almost no support. In November 1916 he reported his latest revolutionary meeting as follows:

> There was a meeting of the Lefts here today: not everybody turned up, only two Swiss and two foreigners, Germans, and three Russian-Jewish-Poles. There was no report, just an informal talk.(16)

Exactly one year later, this isolated, forgotten fanatic was to take Czar Nicholas' place as autocrat of all the Russias, ruler and transformer of one hundred and fifty million people.

* * * * * *

Summer in Portugal, 1916. Heat and light, the mingled scents of tangy earth and sweet blossoms, the mingled colors of red clay, light blue wildflowers, dark green pines, gray-green olive trees, and deep blue sky. In the back country, among the simple sturdy men and women and children who make their living as farmers and shepherds, the world war is little more than a distant rumor, even though Portugal's government has finally been brought into it by British pressure, and is enlisting troops for an expeditionary force.

But there is no conscription; the terrible conflict is far away and scarcely understood, and no Portuguese will reach the front this year. Yet still it is the summer of Verdun and the Somme, the year of two and a quarter million casualties on the Western front.

In the Serra da Aire, the Airy Mountains, rising to modest heights inland from Lisbon, there is a rocky hill known as The Head, commanding a far-ranging view of the Portuguese countryside. The Head is about three miles from the tiny peasant village of Aljustrel, then in the parish of St. Anthony's in the nearby, larger village of Fatima. To The Head, one summer day, three children had come with the sheep they were tending. They often came there, drawn by the beauty of the place and its view, and fascinated by the echoes they could draw from the surrounding hills and rocks. Their names were Lucia Abobora and Jacinta and Francisco Marto. Lucia was the oldest, aged nine. She had received her first Holy Communion; the remarkable extent of her knowledge of the Catholic Faith, for a child of her age with very little formal education, had been attested by the well-known Portuguese Jesuit missionary from Lisbon who had once preached in St. Anthony's Parish, Father Cruz. Jacinta and Francisco were brother and sister, aged six and eight. They loved and followed Lucia, their cousin. She had told them the story of the Passion of Christ, and taught them songs in praise of the Blessed Virgin Mary, Mother of God. The three often prayed the Rosary together during their long days in the fields with the sheep -- though not always completing it -- and Jacinta especially liked to pray it on the Head, loud enough to bring the echoes.

Their faith was simple, direct, profound, and clear to the depths, as in a limpid stream. They called the sun "the lamp of Our Lord" and the moon "the lamp of Our Lady."(17) (Has the most distinguished theologian, Mariologist, or spiritual writer ever found a better symbol for their relationship?) The stars were, to them, the lamps of the angels. Sometimes Jacinta would pick up a very small lamb and carry it around her neck, "to do as Our Lord does," for she had seen the traditional picture (which goes back all the way to the catacombs of Rome) of Him as the Good Shepherd.

> "Let the children come to me, and do not hinder them, for to such belongs the kingdom of heaven."(18)

On this particular summer day a shower accompanied by a
strong wind suddenly descended upon The Head; the children took
shelter from it in a half-cave amid the tumbled rocks. Just after the
shower had ended, they saw a white light in the sky, moving
toward them—not the blue of the sky nor the gold of the sun, but
a pure, vivid, perfect white, in Lucia's later words "like snow that
the sun shines through until it becomes crystalline."(19) (On the
Mount of the Transfiguration, the Gospel of Mark [9:3] tells us,
Jesus' "garments became glistening, intensely white, as no fuller
on earth could bleach them.")

The light took the form of a man, or rather of a boy about
fifteen years of age, translucent, radiant, ineffably beautiful,
inspiring an awe close to fear.

"Don't be afraid," he said, in the ancient, almost universal
introduction of his kind to men, on any first meeting. "I am the
Angel of Peace. Pray with me."

He knelt, then prostrated himself on the ground, and prayed.

> My God, I believe, I adore, I hope, and I love You! I beg
> pardon of You for those who do not believe, do not adore, do not
> hope and do not love You!

He repeated the prayer three times, the enraptured children
repeating it after him. Then he told them: "Pray thus. The hearts
of Jesus and Mary are attentive to the voice of your
supplications."(20)

Then he vanished, in the returning sunlight.

We do not know the precise day the Angel of Peace came to the
Airy Mountains. But we do know that, on any average day that
summer, there were seven thousand futile casualties at Verdun
and on the Somme.

The children told no one then of what had happened, not even
after an angel had come to them twice more that same
summer—one who identified himself as the Guardian Angel of
Portugal, the other who gave Jacinta and Francisco their first Holy
Communion.

The war that came upon the world from 1914 to 1918 was not
only a war of men and nations, generals and armies, monarchs and

revolutionaries. The legions and the powers of Heaven and of Hell were engaged as well, as well-attested events from December 1916 to October 1917 clearly show to those with eyes to see, and ears to hear.

December 30-31, 1916

It was the Christmas season, the time of the birth of God. In the mountain fastnesses and the little hidden valleys of the Tyrol and Styria the glorious nativity sets, the wonder of Austrian folk art, with their hundreds of exquisite figures and houses and animals and scenes all circling about the Christ-Child, were at their places of honor in humble homes, warm and bright with blazing logs. On the plains of Hungary to the east the celebrations were going forward even under the looming shadows of the Great War.

Joy to the world, the Lord has come. . .

On the sixth day of Christmas, December 30, 1916, the city of Budapest, capital of Hungary, witnessed the first coronation that most of its people had ever seen. The streets were decked with arches, flags, flowers, and pictures of the new King and Queen of Hungary. Shortly before nine o'clock in the morning Charles and Zita rode, in a coach drawn by eight superb white horses, through the brilliantly festive ways to the great cathedral of Matthias Corvinus. For Catholic kings are crowned in church, before the Living God Who will judge not only their souls, but their rule.

In an ancient ceremony, hallowed by more than nine hundred years of Magyar history and tradition, the Prince-Primate of Hungary placed upon Charles' head the most cherished treasure of his nation, the Crown of St. Stephen, which Pope Sylvester II had sent to that first Christian monarch of Hungary, to recognize him as such, in the year 1000. Before placing the crown on Charles' head, the Primate touched it to Zita's right shoulder. The coronation cloak which was then wrapped around Charles' shoulders had been embroidered by St. Stephen's Queen, Gisela, in 1031. The newly crowned successor of St. Stephen then came out of the cathedral to take his coronation oath in the great square before it, in the presence of all his Hungarian people who could see and hear him:

> We, Charles IV, by the grace of God perpetual Apostolic King of Hungary and her associated countries, swear by the living God, by the Virgin Mary and all God's saints that . . . we shall not alienate the boundaries of Hungary and her associated countries, nor anything belonging to those countries under any title whatever; shall not reduce but as far as possible increase and extend their territories; and shall do all that we may justly do for the welfare and glory of these our countries. So help us God and His saints.(21)

Then Charles mounted a great gray horse, stirrup and bridle all trimmed with pure gold, and rode to the mound near the palace which contained deposits of earth from every county of Hungary. Atop the mound Charles swung his coronation sword to the four points of the compass, in the ancient form of solemn avowal to defend Hungary against every enemy, from whatever direction he might come. Church bells rang. Artillery salutes roared. Bands played. The people cried: *"Eljen a Kiraly!"* (Long live Charles!") Zita said in remembrance, fifty years later:

> The thing that impressed both of us most about the whole ceremony was the moving liturgical side of it all—especially the oath that the king took at the altar before his anointing to preserve justice for all and strive for peace. This sacred pledge given in the cathedral was exactly the political program he wanted to carry out from the throne. We both felt this so strongly that hardly any words were necessary between us.(22)

A magnificent round of coronation celebrations was planned in Budapest—banquets, formal dress balls, all the glitter of high society. But Charles could not forget the war—the maimed, the dying, the dead. The coronation had moved him to the depths of his being. The prospect of secular festivity seemed inappropriate, at least for him. Charles made it known that he would return to Vienna that very afternoon. He and Zita boarded the train for Vienna in Budapest as the short winter day approached its end. Consciousness of the horrors of war lay heavy upon Charles' heart;

yet we may well imagine that not all the glow of the shared commitment, the royal promise, the consecration of his rule before God, which Zita remembered so well across half a century, had departed. We may guess that from time to time they smiled, that sparkling eyes met, even in the midst of world nightmare, as they thought of the opportunity God had given them to serve Him for the welfare of their peoples, as the train puffed westward through the twilight.

Joy to the world, the Lord has come. . . .Peace on earth to men of good will.

Behind them in Budapest, some of the bells of celebration of a new earthly king, and of the babe who was King of Heaven, were most probably still ringing.

* * * * * *

Night in Petrograd, long black subarctic night, upon blanketing snow and ice. Through the frozen streets a car containing four men was picking its way toward a villa near the edge of the city. In it were the Grand Duke Dmitri Pavlovich, one of the Czar's first cousins;Vladimir Purishkevich, the most ardent monarchist in the Duma; a doctor, S. S. Lazavert; and an army captain, Sukhotin. The house to which they were going belonged to Prince Felix Yusupov, scion of one of the richest noble families of Russia, husband of Czar Nicholas' beautiful niece Irina. The four men had resolved to seek the salvation of Russia, that night, by assassinating Rasputin. It was between eleven o'clock and midnight.

Twenty minutes' drive away, the chief minister of Russia, the absurd Protopopov—Rasputin's creature—was just leaving the house of his mentor, who then dismissed his guard, despite Protopopov's warning that plots were afoot against his life.

Rasputin knew that already. Several days earlier he had written a letter to his secretary Simanovich, a letter written as though from one already dead. It was entitled "The Spirit of Gregory Efimovich Rasputin-Novykh of the village of Pokrovskoe." It predicted his imminent assassination, and said:

If I am murdered by boyars, nobles, and if they shed my blood,
their hands will remain soiled with my blood, for twenty-five
years they will not wash their hands from my blood. They will
leave Russia. Brothers will kill brothers, and they will kill each
other and hate each other, and for twenty-five years there will be
no nobles in the country. Tsar of the land of Russia, if you hear
the sound of the bell which will tell you that Gregory has been
killed, you must know this: if it was your relations who have
wrought my death then no one of your family, that is to say none
of your children or relations, will remain alive for more than two
years. They will be killed by the Russian people.(23)

The car pulled up at Yusupov's luxurious dwelling. The
conspirators met. Yusupov showed them the elaborately decorated
cellar where the assassination was to take place. There were four
bottles of sweet wine and some cakes—three rose, three chocolate.
Dr. Lazavert had brought cyanide, one of the deadliest and
fastest-acting poisons known; a lethal dose kills in seconds, and
may act even through unbroken skin. Therefore Dr. Lazavert put
on rubber gloves before he crushed several cyanide capsules with
a knife, and sifted enough to kill into each of the three rose cakes.
Then he threw the rubber gloves into the fire. He left several more
cyanide capsules with Purishkevich to poison the wine later. Then
Yusupov took the car to go to pick up Rasputin, with Dr. Lazavert
at the wheel, disguised as a chauffeur. Fifteen minutes later
Purishkevich put the remaining cyanide into three glasses of
madeira wine, Rasputin's favorite, and checked his heavy Savage
revolver to make sure that it was loaded.

At one o'clock in the morning of December 31, Yusupov arrived
at Rasputin's house. He had some difficulty gaining admittance at
that hour; then Rasputin took time to comb his beard, for he
thought he was going to meet Yusupov's beautiful wife Irina.
(Actually she was far away, in the Crimea.) He put on a white silk
blouse embroidered with cornflowers, and black velvet pants. His
normally foul body odor was masked by a strong smell of cheap
soap. After half an hour he was finally ready to go, and at two
o'clock in the morning he entered Yusupov's house and was taken
immediately to the cellar. Upstairs a primitive "gramophone"
played raucously, over and over, the rollicking tune of "Yankee

Doodle" as a way of suggesting to Rasputin that the noble ladies
he had come to see were diverting themselves with the music.

Yusupov went down into the cellar alone with Rasputin. He
offered him the rose cakes filled with cyanide. At first he refused
them. Then he ate one, then another.

Nothing happened.

Yusupov gave him an unpoisoned glass of wine, then a
poisoned glass. He drank it, sipping. His hand went to his throat,
and he stood up.

"Is anything the matter?" Yusupov asked.

"Nothing much," Rasputin replied. "Just an irritation in the
throat. . . .That's very good madeira. Give me some more."(24)

Yusupov gave him a second glass of the cyanide-laced wine.
This time Rasputin drained it almost at a single gulp.

Nothing happened.

Then, as Yusupov tells us in his harrowing account of that night
(we have two, one by him and one by Purishkevich):

> All of a sudden his expression changed into one of fiendish
> hatred. Never before had he inspired me with such horror.
> I felt an indescribable loathing for him, and was ready to throw
> myself upon him and throttle him.
> I felt that he knew why I had brought him there, and what I
> intended to do to him. A mute and deadly conflict seemed to be
> taking place between us. I was aghast. Another moment and I
> should have gone under. I felt that confronted by those satanic
> eyes, I was beginning to lose my self-control. A strange feeling
> of numbness took possession of me. My head reeled.(25)

Rasputin's head bent, and fell into his hands. Then he raised
his head, and asked Yusupov to play for him on his guitar, and to
sing him a song.

It was two-thirty in the morning.

Finally Yusupov made an excuse to leave the cellar room, and
hurried upstairs. Dr. Lazavert had fainted from the stress. The
other three all had their revolvers out, and wanted to rush down
together to kill Rasputin. Yusupov dissuaded them. He was
determined to try again, alone. Taking Dmitri's revolver, he went
back down the stairs. Rasputin appeared ill, but quickly improved
after another glass of wine. Yusupov held the revolver behind his
back.

Atop a richly decorated cupboard hung a seventeenth-century crucifix made of rock crystal and silver. Yusupov went over to it. He stood beneath it.

"I love this cross," he said.

Rasputin said the trinkets in the cupboard were more to his fancy.

Yusupov replied: "Gregory Efimovich, you had better look at the crucifix, and say a prayer before it."(26)

For a moment, after he spoke these words, the almost paralyzing fear left Yusupov; Rasputin no longer seemed to have the power to impose it. His almost colorless eyes were fixed on the crucifix.

Yusupov brought the revolver into view and fired. The two men were standing face to face.

Rasputin roared like a wild beast. The crash of his falling body resounded through the house. The conspirators came rushing down the stairs. The body lay on a thick rug made from the fur of a polar bear, white as snow.

They dragged the body off the rug. There was no blood. Even a drop would have showed clearly on the pure white surface. There was only one small red spot on Rasputin's white cornflowered silk blouse.

They examined the bullet wound. It was in the region of the heart. Rasputin was not yet dead, for they could hear his breath rasping and rattling. But he was still, and must be dying.

The conspirators now put into effect their plan to fake a return by Rasputin to his house by having Captain Sukhotin put on Rasputin's coat and hat and drive away in the direction from which he had come, in case the secret police had followed him to Yusupov's house. Grand Duke Dmitri, Dr. Lazavert, and Sukhotin disguised as Rasputin departed in the car, leaving Yusupov and Purishkevich in the house with the murdered man.

Attempting to calm their shaken nerves, Yusupov and Purishkevich smoked and talked. They spoke of a brighter future for Russia, a splendid recovery now that the shadow of Gregory, son of Efim, the Dissolute, had been removed from the imperial throne. Eventually Yusupov went back down to the cellar.

Rasputin was still lying motionless. There was now a little blood, but no pulse. The body was still warm.

Moved by an impulse he could never explain, Yusupov suddenly shook the body violently. The left eyelid fluttered. The left eye opened, then the right—those hypnotic, gray-green eyes—and fastened upon Yusupov a look "of diabolical hatred."

A moment, suspended in time, the darkest and most ancient horrors which haunt the human soul focussed upon Yusupov in that underground room as though by a burning glass—and the body of Rasputin rose up with foaming lips and wild-beast roar, grasping Yusupov by the shoulder in a grip of iron, reaching for his throat, repeating "in a hoarse whisper," over and over, Yusupov's name.

"Felix. . .Felix. . .Felix. . .Felix. . .Felix. . ."

Exerting every ounce of his strength whetted by the utmost extremity of terror, Yusupov tore himself free from the nightmare grip and rushed up the stairs screaming: "Purishkevich! Shoot! Shoot! He's alive! He's getting away!"(27)

For a moment Purishkevich must have thought Yusupov had gone mad. He could think of no response. Then he heard a scrambling sound on the cellar steps.

Rasputin was climbing up on all fours, roaring. For an instant neither of the two men at the top of the stairs could move. They stood stock still, as though paralyzed, as the shape of Rasputin humped and staggered up the last few stairs, across the hall, through the door, and out into the snowy courtyard, saying: "Felix, Felix, I'll tell it all to the Czarina."(28)

It was between three and four o'clock in the morning, the loneliest hour of the night.

Purishkevich was a crack shot. At last he pulled out his Savage revolver and began firing. His first two bullets missed. This scene from Hell was not in the least like the firing range at the Semyonov Barracks where he regularly practiced. The whiplash echo of the futile shots rang through the silent night.

Rasputin scrambled on. He was nearing the only unlocked gate of the courtyard, which opened directly upon the street. He was escaping.

Purishkevich bit his hand to steady himself. He fired again, and again. The bullets struck Rasputin in the shoulder and in the neck. He collapsed in a deep snowdrift, grinding his teeth in rage.

Purishkevich knew the four shots must have been heard. Two soldiers were in the street. He opened the gate, called them over, and told them: "I've killed Grishka Rasputin, enemy of Russia and the Czar."

The two soldiers embraced and kissed him. "Thank God."

He told them not to tell anyone what they had seen and heard.

"Yes, Excellency," they replied. "We are Russian people. Have no doubts of us."(29)

Then they helped him drag the body back into the house.

Repeating, as though in a trance, Rasputin's "Felix . . . Felix . . . Felix," Yusupov, after being violently sick, came back to the body and gazed upon its now blood-spattered and distorted face.

Then he heard a faint whining sound. He saw an eye open. Leaping upon the body in a renewed frenzy of terror and loathing, he beat it frantically with a two-pound leaded walking stick. Purishkevich dragged him away.

Grand Duke Dmitri, Dr. Lazavert, and Captain Sukhotin had now returned in the car. Yusupov and Dr. Lazavert were unmanned by the night of terror; Purishkevich was now in charge. He, Dmitri, and Sukhotin put the body in the car. It had been wrapped in a blue curtain, with a rope bound tightly around both its arms and its legs.

Purishkevich felt the body. It was still warm.

Purishkevich drove to the Petrovsky brige over the Staraya branch of the Neva River. There was a sentry box on the bridge. The sentry was asleep, but the conspirators did not know that. They stopped the car, turned off the engine and the lights, and hurriedly dumped the body head first over the parapet into a hole in the ice kept open by the swift current of the river. On the way down, the tumbling body struck either the bridge abutment, or the ice, or both, breaking its head open. In their hurry the conspirators had forgotten to attach to the body the weights they had brought for this purpose; now they were hastily and loosely attached to Rasputin's coat. One boot was thrown down, but it sailed in the

wind and landed on the ice instead of in the water of the hole. The
other boot lay forgotten in the car.

It was a little after four o'clock in the morning. The world
slept—the great and the simple, the good and the evil, from
Petrograd all across Europe. In Vienna, Charles and Zita; in
Zurich, Lenin and Krupskaya; in Aljustrel near Fatima, Lucia and
Jacinta and Francisco.

The car started up, and drove away from the the Petrovsky
bridge.

Under the black water at the edge of the ice, the shape of
Rasputin bobbed and writhed. The cyanide from three poisoned
cakes, and then from two poisoned glasses of wine, had long since
passed from its stomach to the inner tissues of its body, where it
kills swiftly and unerringly—most surely of all when in a lethal
dose prepared by a doctor. Yusupov's bullet lay near its heart,
Purishkevich's fourth bullet in its neck—both wounds later
pronounced surely mortal by medical examiners. Its head,
battered by the blows of Yusupov's lead-weighted stick, was
broken open in several places by the impact of the head-first fall
from the bridge; blood from the gaping wounds eddied in the
water. Gregory, son of Efim, the Dissolute, the dark angel of
Russia, had already died at least five times that night. Now came
the sixth death—drowning, and freezing. No man, however
healthy, could live more than a few minutes in the ice-choked Neva
River in Petrograd, at sixty degress north latitude, at four o'clock
in the morning on the last day of the year, in the devouring waters
under the polar wind.

The shape moved. It held its breath. It tried to draw breath,
and water began to enter its lungs. But its hands were busy—those
big, fleshy hands with their long thick fingers. The left hand
clenched into a fist, straining against its bonds. The right hand
twisted and turned until it had freed itself entirely from the hastily
knotted rope, whose grip upon left hand and legs alone was still
keeping the body from rising to the surface through the hole in
the ice, and swimming to shore.

The fingers tugged at the bonds and the knots. No man saw it.
No dog howled. There was only the snow and the stillness, white

enveloped by black. It was the eve of 1917, the most fateful year in the history of the world since Christ ascended into Heaven.

The scene fades from our sight. We know no more. Not for our minds and eyes is the last battle in that dark river under the ice, nor may we know from what far realms its ultimate combatants were drawn. The Arctic night closes in, to be followed four hours later by the pale dawn and the pale brief day of the far north in deepest winter. That day Rasputin's boot was found on the ice, and tracks in the snow piled at the edge of the Petrovsky bridge. The authorities began a search on the frozen river the next day, using divers, and policemen traversing the ice. One of the policemen, making a hole in the ice, found Rasputin's fur coat. Two hundred feet from the bridge the body was recovered, entirely encased in ice; but its lungs were full of water, signifying that it had been still alive and trying to breathe underwater, and its right hand was free of the constricting rope, and reaching out.

It was dead at last. But so was Imperial Russia.

January 1917

Czar Nicholas returned to Petrograd to bury Rasputin beneath a small chapel in the Imperial Park on January 3, with an icon in the coffin signed by each member of the royal family. The next day, January 4, his laconic diary tells us that he took "a walk in the dark."

Through all of the next two months Nicholas and Alexandra seemed to be walking in the dark. They seemed immobilized, as though cut off from reality. Alexandra wept almost constantly. They repeated the old formulas, maintaining their determination never to relax the autocracy. But their hearts were not in it—if, indeed, Nicholas' ever had been—nor in anything they were doing. A deadly stillness fell on the fountainhead of the great Russian state.

The stream of warnings, which had flowed so strongly in the fall of 1916, swelled to a flood in the winter of 1917. The warnings came from the Czar's friends, or those who wished to be such; from loyal subjects; even from foreign ambassasdors. Reform was necessary, absolutely necessary, to restore public confidence and to save the Russian state, Nicholas was told again and again. He must show himself to the people, take charge as a reformer, establish responsible government through the Duma. Nicholas listened, smiling politely. He took no action. In the words of the French ambassador, Paleologue, he was as though "swept away by destiny," having already "abdicated in spirit."(30)

The government remained essentially as it had been when Rasputin died. Trepov, already hopelessly compromised by the hostility of Rasputin and Alexandra, was allowed to retire as Acting Premier January 9. Protopopov, as Interior Minister, remained the leading figure in the cabinet, but now totally without direction from above and incapable of offering direction himself. The new premier was the aged, inexperienced and incompetent Prince Golitsyn, who had begged the Czar with tears in his eyes not to appoint him. Nicholas was as unmoved by Golitsyn's humble pleas and tears as he was unmoved by the most vehement warnings of those who besought him for decisive action to save the monarchy and Russia.

For all practical purposes, during January and February of 1917 Russia had no government.

* * * * * *

Cold and deadly as the wolf-haunted Siberian *taiga*, as the snow-wrapped forests between Petrograd and the White Sea, is the North Atlantic Ocean in winter. Westerly storms sweep across it in pitiless succession; periodically among its gray waves appears the white glint of the iceberg. In 1912 the passenger liner *Titanic*, the finest ship of its kind in the world, had gone down with over a thousand of its passengers from the mere nudge of one of these polar monsters. In 1915 the British liner *Lusitania*, carrying 1257 passengers including 440 women and 129 children, and a crew of 702, sank in the North Atlantic with the loss of 1198 lives (including 120 American passengers). But this ship had been "nudged" not by an iceberg, but by a torpedo fired without warning from a submerged German submarine.

The number of victims on the *Lusitania* obviously did not begin to compare with the colossal casualty totals for the Western front, nor the civilian casualities in devastated Belgium. But there was a peculiar, unforgettable poignancy in the deaths of those women and children swallowed by the gray waves, helpless, impossible to save, slain by a hidden enemy against whom they were most assuredly not fighting. The fact, established long afterward, that munitions were carried aboard the *Lusitania* may involve the British government to a significant degree in the moral responsibility for the disaster; it does not change the fact that Germany's methods of submarine warfare had brought this uniquely terrible evil upon the world.

As the winter of 1917 clamped down upon the northern hemisphere, Imperial Germany was preparing its fateful decision to launch unrestricted submarine warfare on all but a very few specially designated ships approaching the British Isles from the North Atlantic, whether or not they were neutral, whatever they might or might not be carrying as passengers or cargo.

Germany's leaders, civilian and military, were desperate—though not desperate enough to make peace. Instead they were prepared to risk everything on their "miracle weapon," the submarine, which Grand Admiral Holtzendorff, Field Marshal Hindenburg, and General Ludendorff had convinced themselves could win the war in six months, before the American intervention which it would inevitably provoke could take effect. The pros and cons of this action—moral, political, military—had been argued all through the two and a half years of the war so far. The Germans had marshalled a battery of arguments: the British were blockading them, preventing even food imports from entering Germany on neutral ships; the submarines were imposing only a counter-blockade, justified if the British blockade was justified; the submarine was so vulnerable that it could not always take the merchant ships by the time-honored method of the "shot across the bows," search for contraband, and seizure or destruction of any contraband found, while insuring the safety of passengers and crew.

In the echo of the dying cries of the women and children on the *Lusitania*, before the prospect of loosing this kind of war indiscriminately upon peaceful ships in the winter North Atlantic, these arguments faded into embarrassed silence, hardly convincing even those who made them, leaving only the blood and iron of old Hindenburg, as he said the night before the meeting with the Kaiser to make the decision on unrestricted submarine warfare: "Things cannot be worse than they are now. The war must be brought to an end by whatever means as soon as possible."(31)

"By whatever means"—except peace.

At Pless castle on the German-Polish border, where Supreme Headquarters of the German army was located, four civilian ministers and Chancellor Bethmann-Hollweg met with Holtzendorff, Hindenburg, Ludendorff, and Kaiser Wilhelm at six o'clock in the evening of January 9. The Kaiser was "pale and excited." Admiral Holtzendorff grandiloquently announced that unrestricted submarine warfare would win the war for Germany before a single American soldier set foot on the European continent. He "guaranteed victory" by this means. Ludendorff insisted on the necessity of action to forestall expected vast Entente spring offensives on the Western front. Bethmann-Hollweg could only warn that America might prove stronger than anyone expected and speak of the generalized dangers of widening a conflict already so immensely destructive. He spoke for an hour, whle the Kaiser—who had long supported him on this issue against the generals and admirals—became increasingly impatient. But in the end the Chancellor concluded: "It is a very grave decision, but if the military authorities regard it as necessary, I am not in a position to contradict them."(32)

The military men were ready with an order already drafted for the Kaiser's signature. They place it before him. He signed it. The order read:

> I command that unlimited submarine warfare begin on February 1 with all possible vigor. You will please take all necessary measures immediately, but in such a way that our intention does not become apparent to the enemy and to neutrals in advance.(33)

The Kaiser, the generals, and the admiral marched out, leaving Bethmann-Hollweg slumped in a chair. An old retainer of the Hohenzollerns, entering the room, came up to him to ask what was wrong.

"*Finis Germaniae*," said the Chancellor of the Second Reich.(34)

Three days later the implementing operational orders went out to Germany's submarine fleet. A week later Bethmann-Hollweg informed Germany's ambassador to the United States of the decision (to be kept strictly secret until the last day of the month)

while Foreign Minister Zimmermann sent along with the
Chancellor's message a telegram in cipher to be passed to
Germany's ambassador in Mexico, offering German help to
Mexico to regain Texas, New Mexico and Arizona from the United
States. The message for Mexico was sent on the U.S. State
Department cable, President Wilson having given the German
government permission to use it even for ciphered messages to aid
in the peace negotiations he was trying to set in motion.

On January 20 Admiral Holtzendorff went to Austria to explain
the decision there. He had already convinced the principal
Austrian military and naval commanders of its necessity, and had
now shortened his estimate of the time in which his submarines
were to win the war, to four months.

Emperor Charles was neither impressed nor convinced. Alone
against them all, he held out. He called Holtzendorff into a private
meeting, pouring out his objections. Finally the Admiral told him
bluntly: "It is too late for argument. Our U-boats are already at sea
with their new orders and a countermand can no longer reach
them."(35)

Charles was appalled. There was nothing he, or anyone, could
do now to reverse the decision. Even the grim Admiral must have
felt the luminous force of the moral disapproval of the young
couple who were heirs to the thousand-year tradition of the Holy
Roman Emperors, the temporal heads of Christendom; for at
dinner that night he turned brutally upon Zita and snapped: "I
know you are an opponent of U-boat warfare. You are against war
altogether."

She replied: "I am against war as every woman is who would
rather see people live in joy than in suffering."(36)

Below the gray seas and the white winds, the U-boats were
making their way to their stations in the North Atlantic on the
western sea approaches to the British Isles.

***** *

Thomas Woodrow Wilson, the former professor who had first
been elected President of the United States when two opponents

split the vote against him and was then re-elected by an eyelash because his opponent forgot to shake the hand of the Governor of California, is one of the most improbable figures in American political hstory. In no sense gregarious, he preferred being alone, or with his family. Of strong convictions, deliberate but firm in his judgments, he was little influenced by advisors. He made his great decisions in solitude, composing his most critical Presidential statements entirely by himself on his battered portable typewriter. He was a proud man, often intellectually arrogant; and he knew very little of Europe. He was to be tested to the utmost, the defects of his virtues pitilessly revealed, and ultimately broken in the shattering aftermath of the First World War. But now, in January 1917, Woodrow Wilson stood for sanity, for reason. Though war hysteria already gripped substantial segments of the American public, a majority favoring the Entente, a minority (mostly of German or Irish extraction) favoring the Central Powers, relatively few Americans actually wanted war, and Wilson certainly did not. He abhorred, and would not accept or endure full-scale submarine war on neutrals and civilians at sea, as he had repeatedly made clear. But he would not take the United States into the war for any lesser reason, and he sincerely sought peace. On January 22, in a major statement to the U.S. Senate, he finally said what no other statesman had dared to say publicly throughout the whole ghastly conflict to this point: There must be "a peace without victory."

> Victory would mean peace forced upon the loser, a victor's terms imposed upon the vanquished. It would be accepted in humiliation, under duress, at an intolerable sacrifice, and would leave a sting, a resentment, a bitter memory upon which terms of peace would rest, not permanently, but only as upon quicksand. Only a peace between equals can last, only a peace the very principle of which is equality and a common participaion in a common benefit.(37)

Wilson was later to convince himself, and much of his country and the world, that a vast gulf deriving from their different forms of government separated the contenders in the war and made the defeat of the Central Powers necessary to keep the world "safe for democracy"—that, in fact, a victor's peace must be imposed upon those powers, their national structure and territory transformed and dismembered, at the risk of all the evil consequences he had warned of on January 22, 1917, all of which in fact came to pass. But at this time he spoke for a far nobler view and truth: that nothing fundamental divided the combatants, that a fair and just peace could be made. Pope Benedict XV called his speech "the most courageous document which has appeared since the beginning of the war. . . .It contains many truths and revives the principles of Christian civilization."(38)

But the belligerents would have none of it. English and French editors and writers poured scorn on "peace without victory." How absurd! How insipid! How unthinkable! Meanwhile, in the German ambassador's desk, the two fatal messages smoldered like fuses on a bomb—the one announcing unrestricted submarine warfare as an irreversible commitment, to begin in ten days; the other calling for an attack on the continental United States. Without victory, all sides insisted more obstinately than ever after two and a half years of the bloodiest war of all time, there would be no peace.

Except for Emperor Charles. Already in the month of January he had begun to put into effect a unique plan for peace negotiations who initial conception went back to the very first days of his reign. It involved Zita's family, the royal house of of his reign. It involved Zita's family, the royal house of Bourbon-Parma, which because of the French origin of the Bourbons, tended to regard itself as French. Because of this, Zita's brothers Sixtus and Zavier were serving as artillery officers in the Belgian army, in order to be fighting by the side of the French. At the beginning of December 1916 Charles asked his mother-in-law, the Duchess of Parma, to make contact with Sixtus and Xavier. On January 29 they met their mother in Neuchatel, Switzerland. She told them that Charles deeply desired to discuss peace terms with them, using them as emissaries to contact the Entente governments, and that he had made all necessary arrangements for bringing them immediately and secretly to Vienna to confer with him. However, if they were not yet willing to come to Vienna, he would send a represenatative to talk with them in Switzerland. Charles stressed to her that time was of the essence. She presented letters to her sons from both Charles and Zita conveying their sense of urgency.

Sixtus and Xavier told their mother they did not believe they should then go the Vienna, but would meet with Charles' representative in Switzerland if the French government approved. Sixtus urged Charles to consider the following terms he regarded as indispensable for a mutually acceptable peace: the restoration of Alsace-Lorraine to France; the restoration of all of Belgium; the restoration of Serbia, extended to include Albania; and the cession of Constantinople to Russia.

On January 31 Germany's decision for unrestricted submarine warfare was conveyed to the U.S. Secretary of State by the German ambassador, and then made public. President Wilson promptly broke diplomatic relations with Germany, but still would not recommend war until an "overt act" in carrying out this policy, had occurred.

February 1917

The first part of the month of February was a period of waiting. The tonnage of British ships sunk by German submarines began to rise, but no neutral ships were attacked at this time—most of them having stayed out of the new war zone the Germans had proclaimed all around the British Isles—nor any passenger liners. The "overt act" for which President Wilson was waiting did not then materialize. A new Austrian ambassador, Count Tarnowski, arrived in Washington about the time the German ambassador, Count Bernstorff, was departing. The American government welcomed Tarnowski and made it clear to him that no immediate break in American diplomatic relations with Austria was anticipated. The Austrian government had seen no way to withhold support from Germany's unrestricted submarine warfare without breaking up the alliance of Austria with Germany before Charles' independent negotiations had developed to the point where that might be necessary, wise or safe; they had even proclaimed Austria's intent to use unrestricted submarine warfare itself in the Mediterranean, where Austria had a modest fleet, but the American government was quite sure Austria had no real intention of doing so. Rather, it was indicated that Austria hoped to serve as a link for peace negotiations between the United States and Germany, now that the regular diplomatic links between those two countries had been broken. Count Czernin, the new Foreign Minister Charles had recently appointed because he was the only one among his principal advisors who consistently favored peace, even notified U.S. Secretary of State Lansing explicitly that Austria accepted President Wilson's formula of "peace without victory."

In Austria February 13, Emperor Charles received Kaiser Wilhelm on a state visit. In their discussions Charles refused Wilhelm's request that Austria break off diplomatic relations with the United States because the United States had severed them with Germany. He also told Wilhelm that he was undertaking a new and important peace initiative to the Entente and obtained his grudging approval, though Charles refused to reveal the names of those with whom he was dealing. That same day, in Neuchatel, Thomas Erdody of the Hungarian police, a childhood friend of Charles, was meeting as his envoy with Sixtus to convey Charles' acceptance of the restoration of Alsace-Lorraine and of Belgium as essential to peace, and his promise to seek an armistice with Russia possibly including a free hand in the disposition of Constantinople. On the thorny issue of Serbia Charles made a counter-proposal for a larger pan-Slav kingdom in the Balkans, self-governing yet under the overall sovereignty of the House of Habsburg. Sixtus held out for the enlarged and wholly independent Serbia to include Albania, so as to give it access to the sea. He also passed on a rather disingenuous request from the French government that Charles immediately sign a unilateral public declaration of a separate peace with the Entente powers and a secret treaty of alliance with them.

Erdody returned to Vienna and consulted with Charles, who realized immediately the trap that was being laid for him. His purpose was most certainly not simply to switch sides in the war, but to end the war. Erdody was sent back to Neuchatel with a discouraging memorandum from Czernin rejecting the idea of a separate peace, a letter from Zita again imploring her brothers to come to Vienna for direct talks, and a letter from Charles together with his annotations and clarifications of Czernin's memorandum. The messages from Charles, delivered by Erdody to Sixtus at Neuchatel February 21, were of the greatest importance, by far the most genuine and unselfish peace offer by the head or government of a belligerent state in the whole course of the war.

Charles explained that he sought peace not only because of "military condition"—the strain and losses of the war—but above all "as his solemn duty, before God, towards the peoples of his

Empire and all the belligerents."(39) (In a tempestuous ocean of aggressive and intolerant nationalism, here at last a concern for *all* Christendom from someone other than the Pope—most fitting in the heir to the Holy Roman Emperors who had been responsible for the temporal welfare of Christendom as a whole.) Charles expressed admiration for the heroic resistance of France and "the greatest sympathy for Belgium," being "well aware that she has been unjustly treated."(40) He then proceeded to offer to join in compensating Belgium for the devastation she had suffered—an astonishing, almost incredible offer, which may well stand alone in the whole history of international relations, and makes nonsense of the charge against Charles' peace initiative that he was simply giving away other people's territory, namely that held or claimed by the Germans. Charles also informed Sixtus through this letter of his recent refusal of the Kaiser's demand that he break diplomatic relations with the United States.

With this now much more fully developed peace initiative, Sixtus returned to Paris to convey it to President Poincare of France. Meanwhile the American ambassador in Vienna, Penfield, passed on an assurance just given by Lloyd George in response to an American request, that the Entente did not aim at the total destruction of the Austrian multinational state, but would permit the union at least of Austria, Hungary, and Bohemia to continue. It was not a sufficient guarantee from Austria's standpoint, but it went further than the Entente had been prepared to go before, and demonstrated a friendly attitude on Wilson's part in striking contrast to his position a year later, when he refused to deal with Charles at all because he was an "unelected ruler."

In the United States, the pause between war storms ended in the last days of February. On February 24 President Wilson received from his ambassador in London the full text of the Zimmermann telegram urging Mexico to attack the United States, obtained by British Naval Intelligence which had long ago broken the German cipher; on February 27 the President was given irrefutable proof that the telegram had actually been transmitted on the U.S. State Department cable he had trustingly allowed the German ambassador to use, supposedly for peace negotiations. And on February 26 Wilson went before a joint session of Congress to ask for authority to arm American merchant ships for protection against submarine attack. While he was speaking to Congress, the news came into the chamber that the British passenger liner *Laconia* had been torpedoed without warning by a German submarine off Ireland. The crew was efficient, the Irish coast was not far away, and all but twelve of the nearly 300 passengers aboard were saved in lifeboats. But two of the dead were American women, Mrs. Mary Hoy and her daughter. They had died of exposure in the open boats in the February North Atlantic, on the way to wind-whipped Bantry Bay. Mrs. Hoy's son telegraphed President Wilson directly "asking him as an American citizen that the death of my mother and sister be avenged."

Wilson ordered the publication of the Zimmermann telegram (whose authenticity the German Foreign Minister soon afterward publicly admitted) and, following his second inauguration March 5, went into almost complete seclusion for two weeks, to prepare his case for America's entry into the war.

March 1917

In Petrograd, by the old calendar that went all the way back to Julius Caesar, the early days of March were still February; by any calendar, it was still winter—Petrograd's subarctic winter, when the temperature fell as low as forty degress below zero by the Fahrenheit scale. Transportation had largely broken down during the fiercely cold January, greatly aggravating the late winter food shortages which always threaten in a far northern climate. Czar Nicholas, still almost oblivious to the world around him, was about to leave for army headquarters at Mogilev.

In the numbing cold of three o'clock in the morning the bread lines began to form. Russian women, wrapped in every layer of clothing they had and could put on, even their faces covered against the serious danger of frostbite, stood patient, enduring, in the bitter polar wind. It was four hours to dawn, six hours until the bakeries opened. For hour after frozen hour they suffered, waiting—only to be greeted, more often than not, by a two-word sign hurriedly posted by a fast-disappearing baker (for shopkeepers had been beaten by those who had waited long hours for them to open their shops, and found nothing there): *khleba nyet*, "no bread."

In store after store there was no flour, no sugar, no meat, no candles, no kerosene. In the freezing apartments there was almost no wood for the stoves and fireplaces. What little there was of all these things, the fortunate few among a population swollen by war to two and a half million, quickly snapped up.

"How can we live like this?" the huddling women asked.(41)

No one had any answer.

On March 8 there was an immense line of women at every

bakery in Petrograd, crying out for bread. The incompetent government of Golitsyn and Protopopov was fumbling toward a rationing system. The government seized much of the small remaining supply of flour in order to have bread to distribute under the new rationing. Among the supplies seized was all the flour held by the Petrograd Consumers Society to bake bread for the eating places of the city's factory workers and workers cooperatives, where more than 125,000 people—including many of the workers' families—ate every day.

No bread at home, no bread at work.

At the Putilov steel factory, the largest industrial establishment in Russia, which employed over 26,000 workers, there had been a strike March 2 and a lockout March 6. Now the factory was closed for lack of fuel. Its workers were in the streets. The night before, a delegation from the Putilov factory had come to see the fiery young orator they called the "Citizen Deputy" in the Duma, Alexander Kerensky. They had warned him that their strike was revolutionary in its purpose; they intended to launch a mass movement against the entire regime.

The strikers marched to the Duma, then to the Cathedral of Our Lady of Kazan. They were solemn, resolute, orderly. Other strikers joined them. Two large bakeries were sacked that day by the women who had been in line before them.

The Czar's departure for Mogilev, some five hundred miles away, left General Sergei Khabalov in command in Petrograd. He issued a reassuring proclamation: there was plenty of bread on hand, the only problem was that "many people fearing a shortage have bought it to put away as hard tack."(42) The bakers immediately sent a delegation to the general. We have no flour, they told him, for bread, for "hard tack," or anything else.

Khabalov called up the Cossacks of the First Don Regiment.

These world-famous centaurs were the pride of the Russian cavalry. Drawn from the descendants of generations of soldiers settled in the southeastern frontier regions of Russia, primarily in the wild prairies between the Black and the Caspian Seas where the Don River flows, with a highly distinctive tradition and way of life, they were born to the military profession; every Cossack village had to supply a large regular quota of cavalrymen. Having little in common either with the toiling peasants or city dwellers (Cossacks did not live in cities), they were uniquely valuable as defenders of the Czar and the Russian state, supposedly immune to the weaknesses of citizen soldiers and the blandishments of agitators.

But the Don Cossacks were men. They too had suffered, as all had suffered in Petrograd during that terrible winter, not only physically but spiritually, in a miasma void of purpose and hope. They no longer served a man, but a shadow of a man; they no longer served a state, but the hollow shell of a state, ready to crack at a touch; and everyone knew it.

The crowds of strikers and demonstrators cheered the Cossacks, while still shouting for bread. "Push harder," some Cossacks told the people, "and we'll let you through."(43)

That night a blizzard halted most of the trains coming into Petrograd, some of them carrying flour and other supplies.

On March 10 the people shut down the city. Every factory was closed. No public transportation ran. Stores were looted. Signs appeared: "Down with the German woman [the Empress]! Down with Protopopov! Down with the War!" Mass meetings were held. At three o'clock in the afternoon a police officer named Krylov led what seemed to be a charge of mounted police against the mass meeting that had been going on all day in Znamenskaya Square. One of the Don Cossacks raised his pistol and shot him dead.

That night the Czar, by telegram from Mogilev, commanded Khabalov to "end the disorders in the Capital" on the following day, firing on the crowds if necessary.

With perhaps a quarter of a million people, hungry and angry, in the streets, and the troops unruly and of low quality, this was not going to be easy. Nor did Khabalov, a wholly undistinguished officer suddenly plunged into one of the supremely critical moments of history, have the slightest idea how to go about it.

"What do I do?" Khabalov wailed. "How do I end it tomorrow?. . .The Czar orders: 'You must fire.' I would be killed. Positively killed."(44) He decided to give the crowds three warnings before shooting.

The Council of Ministers and Khabalov met from midnight to four o'clock in the morning of March 11. Duma President Rodzyanko said Premier Golitsyn should resign. Premier Golitsyn said Protopopov should resign. Protopopov said the Duma should be dissolved. In the end no one resigned, nor was anything of significance done.

Sunday morning, March 11, Petrograd was quieter. (Sunday morning in Holy Mother Russia was traditionally a quiet time, God's time.) In the afternoon a unit of the Pavlovsky regiment opened fire on the people before the Cathedral of Our Lady of Kazan; another unit of the same regiment mutinied and fired on the police; the crowds killed the regimental commander. At Znamenskaya Square, scene of the shooting of Officer Krylov the preceding day, the Volynsky regiment opened fire on the crowd with machine guns. There were volleys into the crowds along the Neva River.

Michael Rodzyanko, president of the Duma, was a bluff, outspoken man of complete integrity and outstanding courage, with a massive build and a booming voice. For years he had striven, with deathless loyalty, to warn his sovereign of the growing and now enormous dangers engulfing him and Russia. Rodzyanko had made every effort to expose Rasputin (who had once unsuccessfully tried to hypnotize him); after Rasputin's death, no one had worked harder than Rodzyanko to arouse and warn the Czar. Late in January he had told him frankly, to his face: "There is not a single honest or reliable man left in your entourage; all the best have either been eliminated or resigned, and only those with bad reputations have remained. . . .The heart of the Russian people is tortured by the foreboding of awful calamities."(45)

Now, on the evening of March 11, Rodzyanko telegraphed the Czar:

> Situation serious. Anarchy in the capital. Government paralyzed. Transport of food and fuel in full disorder. Popular discontent growing. Disorderly firing in the streets. Some military units fire on one another. Essential immediately to order persons having the confidence of the country to form new government. Delay impossible. Any delay deadly. I pray to God that in this hour the blame does not fall on the crown.(46)

Handed this telegram, which proved to be his very last advance warning of ultimate disaster, Nicholas responded: "Once again that fat Rodzyanko has written me some kind of rubbish which I am not even going to answer."(47)

The Czar's answer came in another way. Instead of calling on the Duma to form a government in association with him, that night he suspended its sessions by imperial *ukase.*

That same evening the men of the Volynsky regiment, some of whom had fired the machine guns which had swept the crowd in Znamenskaya Square that afternoon, gathered to talk and argue about what they had done, and might well be called upon to do again the next day. More and more of the Volynsky soldiers assembled. They were off duty, so there were no officers present. The talk grew heated. Full speeches began to be made. For duty, or for revolution? For General Khabalov, or for the insurgent people of Petrograd? For the Czar, or for those who were rejecting him?

Three years ago, two years or one, no thought of any choice but the first of all of these would have entered the minds of any significant number of ordinary Russian soldiers like these men. But they debated only a few blocks away from the icy river where Rasputin had died at last, only a little more than two months before; as some other ordinary soldiers were to demonstrate unmistakably later that month, they had not forgotten Rasputin and what he had done and been allowed to do. And that afternoon, on command, they had mowed down with their machine guns men—and probably some women—driven into formless rebellion simply by lack of bread in the dead of winter.

The heart and backbone of every army is its veteran non-commissioned officers. The commissioned officer usually comes down to his men from higher levels of society; often he really does not know or understand them well, nor they him. This was especially true in Imperial Russia. The sergeant rises from the ranks to lead his men personally into combat, sharing everything with them. With "anarchy in the capital" and "government paralyzed," the Volynsky regiment listened to its sergeants. By six o'clock in the morning of March 12, after an all-night debate, one of them had emerged as its leader. His name was Timofeyev Kirpichnikov. He makes his mark upon the history of the world at this one explosive, pivotal moment. With Sergeant Kirpichnikov, the Volynsky regiment agreed not to fire again on the people of Petrograd.

The officers of the regiment entered the barracks at 6 a.m. Instead of saluting, the soldiers shouted "Hurrah!" Commander Lashkevich asked another of the sergeants present, Markov, what this meant. Markov replied: "It's a signal to disobey your orders!"(48)

The two officers fled outside the barracks. Sergeant Markov and a private went to a window with their rifles, took aim, and fired, killing Lashkevich instantly.

General Khabalov, told of the murder by some breathless messenger just a few minutes after it happened, rushed to the barracks, where he found armed soldiers drawn up in formation—not only the Volynsky regiment under Sergeant Kirpichnikov's command, but two other regiments as well. Wholly lacking in the raw courage and the charisma of leadership that has sometimes quelled such mutinies despite overwhelming odds, unnerved by the rapidly spreading disintegration of his army, Khabalov hurried away as fast as he had come. He wrote out a proclamation of martial law, but could find no glue to post it up.

One of the regimental bands of the rebel units struck up a tune. The mutineers marched out of their barracks into the streets, into the city, carrying red flags. At ten o'clock in the morning they broke into the Liteiny Arsenal, from which they took and distributed no less than 70,000 firearms to the eagerly waiting crowds.

Revolution had come to Russia.

Meanwhile the Czar's order suspending the Duma had arrived. Rodzyanko sent one last telegram to the ruler he still honored and loved:

> The last bulwark of order has been eliminated. The government is absolutely powerless to suppress disorders. Nothing can be hoped from the troops of the garrison. The reserve battalions of the guard regiments are in rebellion. Officers are being killed.

. . . Cancel your Imperial Ukase, and order the reconvening of
the legislative chambers. . . . On behalf of all Russia I beg Your
Majesty to fulfill the foregoing. The hour which will decide the
fate of yourself and of the homeland has come. Tomorrow it may
already be too late.(49)

It was already too late. By noon March 12 there were at least
25,000 fully armed mutineer soldiers in the streets of Petrograd,
along with numerous armed civilians, while Khabalov had been
able to collect only 1500 willing to stand with him. A
brigadier-general was killed by his men. Court buildings, prisons,
and police headquarters were burned or sacked. All around and
among the soldiers roiled a vast throng of ordinary people—
workers, women, adolescents, a cross-section of society below the
aristocrats. A human wave, crested by red flags, singing the
French Revolutionary hymn "La Marsaillaise," they came rolling
up and into the Tauride Palace where the Duma, no longer legally
authorized, was still meeting, at one-thirty in the afternoon.

The wave filled the many rooms and halls of the vast palace to
overflowing. There were at least fifty thousand men. Kerensky
shouted to his Duma colleagues, over the din: "I must know what I
can tell them. Can I say that the Imperial Duma is with them, that
it takes the responsibility on itself, that it stands at the head of the
government?"(50)

Rodzyanko, desperately torn, caught in a rip-tide of history
such as few men have ever had to face, said: "I don't want to
revolt." But his friend Shulgin, who had been as loyal to the
monarchy as he, told him bluntly: "Take the power. If you don't,
others will."(51) So Rodzyanko told the mob that the Duma would
establish a government. But it was already too late for him as well.
The leader of the hour was Kerensky. His oratorical ability and the
impression of decisive, quick-thinking command he had created
during that one wild day made him instantaneously the dominant
figure in the new regime.

For the old regime was dead, dead beyond even the glimmer of
a hope of revival or recall. Never in history has a monarchy fallen
so quickly, so utterly, as the Czarist colossus in March 1917. On
the 15th, three days after the day of revolution in Petrograd, after

one futile, fumbling, farcical attempt to regain the capital with an absurdly small detachment brought from the front, Nicholas abdicated in favor of his brother, Grand Duke Michael. Michael then abdicated the next day. Even among those who later resisted the revolution to the death, among the White armies which fought the Communists for three long, heroic years, there was no support for the Romanov dynasty; not a single member of it played a significant part in the resistance. For Nicholas and Alexandra and their children, there remained only the grim road to Siberian captivity, the road the Ekaterinburg (now Sverdlovsk) and the basement room in its "house of special designation" where, in July 1918, every one of them was murdered in cold blood by revolver shots fired point-blank, whereupon their seven bodies were dismembered, burned, ravaged by acid, and dumped into a mine shaft.

As for their nemesis, his dark memory lived on in the minds of the people; on March 23 they carried out their own crude exorcism. Once again it was in the small hours of the morning. A group of soldiers dug up Rasputin's coffin from the earth beneath the little chapel in the Imperial Park and took it to a clearing in the forest, where they assembled a huge pile of pine logs. They levered out body out of the coffin with sticks; no one wanted to touch it. The body was put on the logs, drenched with gasoline, and set ablaze. It burned for no less than six hours; its ashes were scattered through the silent glades by the frigid wind.

When the mob of fifty thousand had surged into the Tauride Palace March 12, while Kerensky was haranguing and Rodzyanko struggling with his conscience and his sense of duty to Russia, a group of seasoned, hard-eyed revolutionaries was meeting in Room 13 of that same palace to create a mechanism for taking control of this wholly unplanned and unexpected revolution. The idea for such a mechanism already existed, for the rebels of 1905 had formed a Soviet, or council, in Petrograd made up of one elected representative for every thousand factory workers. Some Petrograd workers during the past few days had already elected delegates similarly. Now, in the midst of the boiling confusion at the Tauride Palace, a meeting of a provisional Soviet was called for seven o'clock that very night, in Catherine Hall at the palace. Astonishingly, under the circumstances, the announcement was satisfactorily distributed and the meeting actually held with some 250 delegates present, including the leading Bolshevik then in Moscow, Shlyapnikov, who was named to the Executive Committee of the Soviet, and the young Bolshevik Vyacheslav Scriabin—called Molotov, "hammer"—who made the vital motion that soldiers as well as factory workers should send delegates to the Soviet.

So it was done. On March 14 the famous Military Order Number One, along with virtually destroying military discipline and the authority of officers over the Russian armed forces, provided for the election of soldiers' deputies to the Soviet, one per company. The number of delegates to the Soviet swelled to one thousand, then to almost two thousand. Virtually none of the delegates had the slightest experience in any legislative or deliberative body. Now they were catapulted into a crucible of history, striving and struggling to understand and to act, but rudderless, lost in a strange new world.

By March 15 there were two governments in Russia, operating out of the same building in uneasy and precarious alliance. One was the "Provisional Government" set up by the old Duma, with Prince Lvov, one of the few popular aristocrats, prime minister; Paul Milyukov, leader of the Constitutional Democrats, great friend of Great Britain and France, and strong supporter of the continuation of the war, Minister of Foreign Affairs; and Kerensky Minister of Justice. It was called "provisional" because it was intended, along with discharging the day-to-day functions of government in the meantime, to arrange for and supervise elections to a national parliament, the Constituent Assembly, which would then set up the permanent order of the new Russian state. Beside the Provisional Government was the Executive Committee of the Soviet, almost entirely Marxist, claming to be the only authentic voice of the people, committed not only to the revolution that had already taken place—which was as far as the Provisional Government went—but to broadening and deepening it.

The news spread rapidly across Russia and around the world. A parallel rising, ultimately successful after a week of hard fighting, occurred in Moscow. From the Lena and the Yenisei and the Ob, the far frozen Arctic rivers of Siberia, the political exiles came streaming back—among them, scarcely noticed, a lean hard mustached man with a soft, husky voice from Georgia in the Causasus, Josef Vissarionovich Djugashvili, whose Bolshevik party name was Stalin. At a seedy, $18 per month single room on 164th Street in the Bronx, where he wrote for New York's daily paper for the Russian colony, hawk-faced, smooth-talking Lev Davidovich Bronstein heard the news; within two weeks he had boarded a ship for Russia, where he was known among the Bolsheviks as Trotsky. And in staid Zurich, early in the afternoon of March 16, a young Polish Marxist came rushing into Lenin's apartment, crying: "There's a revolution in Russia!" Lenin and Krupskaya ran to the lovely lake front where newspapers were sold, to buy every one that mentioned the titanic events in Petrograd.

History's deadliest revolution-maker now had his supreme opportunity—if only he could get back to his native land through the encircling ring of warring nations.

******

On March 6 Prince Sixtus had been received by President Poincare of France, who was much impressed by the evident sincerity and scope of Emperor Charles' peace proposals, though he expressed concern about the Italian reaction, since Italy was an ally of the Entente, actively engaged in battle with Austria, with many claims on Austrian territory by which she set great store, none of which were mentioned in the peace terms so far proposed by Charles and Sixtus. However, Poincare reassured Sixtus, while Italy would have to be consulted at some point in the negotiations, she would not have a dominant voice especially in view of the military incapacity the Italians had so far displayed in the war.

Poincare then conferred with Briand and French Foreign Minister Cambon. All agreed that they needed a written signed statement from Emperor Charles of the minimum terms he would accept on the four points already discussed, which should then be communicated to England and Russia, followed by an armistice with Austria, after which the Italian and Rumanian claims could be negotiated at a peace conference. On March 8, a little before five o'clock in the afternoon, Prince Sixtus saw Poincare again for half an hour, during which Poincare presented him with these requests. The next step was to obtain the written peace offer from Charles. Communicating it to England would be easy, communicating it to Russia a longer and more difficult task. Would Prince Sixtus undertake it himself, going directly to the Czar both on behalf of his brother-in-law Charles, and of the government of France? Prince Sixtus said he would go. Poincare admonished him to speak of this matter only to the Czar in person.

There was no time; for this was the day the bread riots began in Petrograd. Nicholas II had exactly one week left to reign.

On March 19, in the evening, Sixtus and Xavier met Erdody in Geneva. They talked until three o'clock in the morning of the 20th. Erdody had an urgent message from Charles: this time, the princes *must* come to Austria. "One hour of conversation between us will do more to bring about peace than twenty letters spread over six months."(52) Charles promised secrecy and safety in the journey. Erdody joined his personal plea to his master's. Then he handed the princes a letter from their sister. Zita wrote:

> Do not let yourselves be deterred by considerations which might
> in the ordinary way justify you in refusing. Think of all the poor
> men who are in the living hell of the trenches. and are being
> killed by hundreds daily: and come.(53)

On the evening of March 20 the two princes left Geneva with Erdody. Crossing Switzerland, they reached the Austrian frontier the next day. There they were met by the colonel in command of the frontier police, acting on Emperor Charles' personal orders, who secretly let them through, provided them with a car, and accompanied them to Vienna. It had begun to snow heavily. All the day and all the next day it snowed. The car struggled through the drifted roads. In the evening of March 22 they arrived at Erdody's house in Vienna, but there was little time for rest. They

were back in the car at six o'clock the next morning. It was still
pitch dark and snowing heavily, with a fierce wind blowing. Their
destination was Laxenburg Castle a few miles from Vienna, near
the Hungarian border, where Charles and Zita were staying. The
car drew up in an outer courtyard. An elderly captain of the guard,
long in the imperial service, led them to the castle, giving the
password to each sentry standing muffled against the weather.
They passed through a small side door leading to a back staircase
ascending to the royal apartments. The colonel of the frontier
guards, the captain of the palace guard, and Erdody remained on
watch outside; the princes entered the apartments.

Zita's had always been an exceptionally close as well as an
exceptionally large family—her father had twenty children by two
marriages. She has recounted with joy their travels and good times
together during her childhood. She had not seen her brothers since
the war broke out; ever since they had been fighting on the
opposite side from her husband. In this room, now, at the
Laxenburg Palace, was a human microcosm of the tragedy of the
First World War for all Christian Europe—and the love that alone
could overcome that tragedy. We can only imagine the embraces,
the laughter and the tears, for of these Sixtus, in his restrained
account of this extraordinary meeting, does not speak; but of his
brother-in-law the Emperor Charles he says he "found him just as
affectionate, just as fair and as loyal to them as in the old days, but
grave, almost melancholy, with a few white hairs already on his
temples."(54) (He was not yet thirty years old, and had been
Emperor just four months.)

Charles said to them:

> It is absolutely essential that peace be made: and I am willing
> to make it at any cost. This is a fit and propitious time, for all
> countries have experienced success and failure, and there is now
> almost a balance of the opposing forces. It is evident that, if the
> war continues indefinitely, one side may come to win a complete
> victory, and may succeed in crushing its adversary. But can any
> nation ever crush another completely, and, if so, what would the
> price of victory be?(55)

Zita then left the room. Charles and the two princes settled
down to the discussion on which the fate of Europe and of Western

civilization might well depend.

Charles said he intended to make one last effort to convince Germany, his ally, to make peace; if it failed as all other such efforts had failed, he would make a separate peace. He had little hope of success with the Germans; "they all seem to be bewitched," he said.(56) First it was essential to arrive at an understanding with France, England, and Russia on acceptable peace terms. On Alsace-Lorraine and Belgium there was already full agreement on his part with the Entente position. The recent events in Russia had made it unnecessary to retain the previous proposals relating to the transfer of Constantinople from Turkey to Russia. Regarding Serbia, Charles was now ready to agree, saying:

> By a series of misunderstandings, intensified by the stupidity of diplomats, we have succeeded in establishing on our borders a small but most aggravating enemy. This cannot continue. We are prepared to allow her soon to expand, with the whole coast of Albania as an outlet to the sea. In this way Serbia may recover her greatness, and we are only too ready to help her.(57)

Regarding Italy, Charles and his brothers-in-law realized that here was "the reef on which their negotiations might yet be shipwrecked."(58) They agreed that the proper procedure to follow was the one Poincare had suggested: to obtain agreement first with England, France, and Russia, and only after that with Italy. Charles warmly recalled the loyalty and devotion of "his gallant Tyrolese" with whom he had fought the Italians in Friuli. The magnificent mountains and valleys of the Tyrol, the ultimate heart of Austria, had been ever the last refuge of the Habsburgs in time of trouble; the southern half of the Tyrol projected into Italy, and part of it was claimed by the Italians. It was clear how difficult it would be for Charles to relinquish any of it.

Count Czernin was now summoned. He remained only about twenty minutes, speaking coldly and vaguely. It seemed he disapproved of the princes' presence at the castle, and they in turn were not sure how much he could be trusted. Zita then returned to spend a few more minutes with her brothers. Charles asked them to return the next day, and they left as cautiously as they had come. The snow had stopped during the conference; now, as Sixtus put it, "the whole town of Vienna lay silent beneath the snow."(59)

The next morning the princes saw Czernin in Vienna, finding him very dubious about the idea of making a separate peace and very much concerned with preserving complete secrecy regarding their visit to Austria. He did, however, pledge his support for Charles' proposals. That night the princes returned to Laxenburg, where Charles gave them the requested autograph letter specifically setting forth his peace terms as he had explained them the preceding day. The letter concluded:

> Trusting that we may soon be able to put an end to the suffering of all the millions of men and all their families, who are now oppressed by sorrow and anxiety, I beg you to be assured of my most warm and brotherly affection.(60)

Bearing this precious document, the princes left Vienna March 25 and were back in Paris by the 30th. There they found that the Briand government had fallen, to be replaced by a new ministry under the ineffectual octogenarian Alexandre Ribot. But President Poincare was still sympathetic; and, for his part, Charles on March 28 asked Kaiser Wilhelm for a meeting to include their respective foreign ministers, at Homburg vor der Hohe April 3.

Overwhelming events now impended. During the first ten days of April, the United States declared war on Germany; final plans were made for a new French offensive on the Western front which would add 150,000 more futile casualties from France alone, in just three weeks, to the millions already suffered, and drive the French army into mass mutinies; and the German government sent Lenin to Russia on a sealed railway train to make his revolution.

April 1917

The first day of April in 1917 was Palm Sunday, the beginning of Holy Week for most of the Christian world. (It was a week later in Russia.) From Bethany where Jesus Christ had at last found a place to lay His head, in the dwelling of Lazarus and Martha and Mary who may have been Mary Magdalene, to Jerusalem over the brow of the Mount of Olives, the annual Palm Sunday procession wended its way on the route of the Lord—smaller than usual, with few of the pilgrims who ordinarily came from abroad to join it, for the war was now in Palestine too, its Turkish rulers struggling to hold it against a British offensive out of Egypt, now being engaged at Gaza. In Europe's churches the faithful gathered to honor the King of Kings, hailed this day so long ago by the people He had come to save. But in the churches of the United States of America, the words from the pulpit were mostly words of war; pastors too were caught up in the tide of patriotic and bellicose emotion. Only the doctrinaire pacifists still resisted; one of them, Rev. John Haynes Holmes of the Church of the Messiah at Park Avenue and Thirty-fourth Street in New York, after proclaiming his opposition to all war, had the courage to say: "In this church, if nowhere else, the Germans will still be included in the family of God's children."(61) The trustees of the the Church of the Messiah expressed their vehement disagreement with the sermon to newspaper reporters.

Woodrow Wilson, like every statesman, knew far too much of human reality to be a doctrinaire pacifist. But he still included the Germans in the family of God's children. He understood the consequences of a declaration of war. Almost all Saturday night he had been awake, sitting on the south portico of the White House in the gentle night breezes of a Washington spring, working on the draft of his war message to the special session of Congress he had summoned for Monday, April 2. At one o'clock in the morning of Monday, Frank Cobb of the New York *World* arrived to talk with the President. He found him sitting in his study, his long lined face heavy, his famous portable typewriter before him. It had obviously been a long time since he had slept. Cobb reports:

> He said he couldn't see any alternative, that he had tried every way he knew to avoid the war . . . I told him his hand had been forced by Germany, that so far as I could see we couldn't keep out. . . . "Yes," he said, "but do you know what that means? . . . It would mean that we shold lose our heads along with the rest, and stop weighing right and wrong." . . . The President said a declaration of war would mean that Germany would be beaten and so badly beaten that there would be a dictated peace, a victorious peace.
>
> "It means," he said, "an attempt to reconstruct a peace-time civilization with war standards, and at the end of the war there will be no bystander with sufficient power to influence the terms. There won't be any peace standards left to work with. There will be only war standards."(62)

That evening Woodrow Wilson stood before a wildly cheering Congress to bring the United States of America into the war that was destroying the world. His justification was twofold: first, that Germany had already made war on the United States by its submarines (the American merchantman *Aztec* had been torpedoed off Ushant, at the tip of France, only the day before); secondly, "to make the world safe for democracy" and more, to impose democracy on the world. The American political system was to be the standard of right and justice. There was in Woodrow Wilson a deep need to include more than considerations of immediate practical and military necessity in calling for U.S. entry into the war—a need to proclaim for that entry some transcendent purpose, some universal and noble goal. But such a purpose and goal was precisely what this ghastly war had always lacked. Wilson's attempt to invent one was to have immensely destructive consequences, especially for those nations and peoples whose traditions did not harmonize with what Americans regarded as "democracy." Yet he acted, then, in the utmost good faith, summing up the agony of his decision and his visualization of the good he dreamed of flowing from it, toward the end of his address:

> It is a fearful thing to lead this great peaceful people into war, into the most terrible and disastrous of all wars, civilization itself seeming to be in the balance. But the right is more precious than peace, and we shall fight for the things which we have always carried nearest our hearts—for democracy, for the right of those who submit to authority to have a voice in their own governments, for the rights and liberties of small nations, for a universal dominion of right by such a concert of free peoples as shall bring peace and safety to all nations and make the world itself at last free.(63)

"The world itself at last free.". . . The principal historical consequence of World War I was to be the establishment, as far into the future as human eyes can see, of the most fearful, pervasive, far-flung tyranny in the history of mankind—a tyranny so gigantic and so evil that, in the end, only the Mother of God in person can conquer it.

* * * * * *

The day after President Wilson delivered his war message to the United States Congress, two conferences immensely important to the future course of the war were held in Paris and in Homburg vor der Hohe, Germany. The German conference was between the two Emperors, Wilhelm and Charles; the Paris conference concerned the planned new French offensive on the Western front.

While General Gallieni had won the crucial Battle of the Marne in 1914, a combination of professional jealousy and absurdly inflexible military retirement laws had kept him from high command afterward. Joseph Joffre, the French commander-in-chief until the end of 1916, was a French version of Britain's Douglas Haig. After hurling his troops relentlessly and fruitlessly into the cannon's mouth and the machine gun's traverse for more than two years, thereby becoming personally responsible for the useless death or maiming of over a million of his countrymen, he was relieved by Robert Nivelle. Such was the hideous irony, the black humor of this war that Nivelle had gained his military fame and fortune, causing him to be vaulted over the heads of numerous generals of greater distinction and experience, solely by taking two forts at the end of the battle of Verdun which the Germans had captured at the beginning of it—clearly a striking victory by the standards of World War I.

As soon as he took over the supreme command, Nivelle began planning a new offensive, against the large German salient in the Arras-Soissons area. Within a few weeks he had so committed himself to this undertaking, and his vast new authority had gone so much to his head, that he remained totally unconcerned when in February the Germans, recognizing the dangers of their exposed salient, simply removed it by a strategic withdrawal to straighten their lines. He remained equally unconcerned by the fact, reported to him from a dozen different sources, that the Germans were in possession of every major element in his assault plan.

The Minister of War in the Briand government was General Lyautey, probably the greatest colonial administrator France ever produced, and an excellent, level-headed field commander. Lyautey had heard Nivelle's repeated boasts of how his offensive would break the whole German line by the use of a "new army" of "reserves" to exploit the breaches made by the initial attacks of his shock troops. Pressing Renouard, a staff officer, Lyautey finally learned that this reserve army which was to win the battle and break the three-year deadlock on the Western front was to be almost entirely "drawn, during the actual fighting, from the attacking troops themselves."

"But surely, Renouard," bellowed the astounded Lyautey, "this is a plan for the Grand Duchess of Gerolstein!"

After some further pressure Renouard broke down in tears.

"General, I think as you do," he said. "It is mad."(64)

It seemed everyone in authority knew that, but still no one could stop Nivelle. The Briand government had fallen in March, and Lyautey with it; the Ribot government, with Paul Painleve, and aircraft designer, as Minister of War, was now experiencing the same doubts and the same helplessness. On April 3 Ribot and Painleve, the Navy Minister, the Minister of Armaments, and Minister of Colonies Andre Maginot (he of later Line fame) met with Nivelle at the War Ministry in Paris to urge him to reconsider. The entry of the United States into the war promised massive aid in the future; why not wait for it? Nivelle would not hear of doubt or delay. He professed himself sublimely confident of success. He would advance ten kilometers a day. He had the key Craonne plateau "in his pocket." His only problem would be "to hold the troops back once they got started."(65) There would certainly be no repeat of the Somme battle; he most emphaticaly guaranteed it.

An octogenarian, an airplane designer, a seaman, a munitions maker, and Maginot of the Line could find among themselves neither the knowledge nor the strength to oppose such dashing professional optimism. They broke up, concluding "that there had been reached as complete an agreement as circumstances permitted."(66)

Three days later, on Good Friday, confronted with a stream of warnings of the suicidal character of the Nivelle offensive from mostly anonymous or disguised military sources, Painleve tried again, holding another conference, this time in President Poincare's railway car at Compiegne, with the army group commanders present along with Nivelle. But some of the commanders feared to oppose Nivelle to his face before the government, supporting him despite personal conviction to the contrary; others declined to speak at all. Nivelle threatened to resign immediately if not fully supported. Poincare, Ribot, and Painleve crumbled at once, begging him to stay. The offensive would go on.

It was on that same Good Friday, April 6, 1917, that, all speechmaking completed, the United States House of Representatives, following the Senate, declared war on Germany by a vote of 373 to 50.

Meanwhile Emperor Charles and Kaiser Wilhelm had met at Homburg. In a last attempt to persuade the Kaiser to give up Alsace-Lorraine to France—an indispensable prerequisite for peace—Charles offered to give Germany the whole of Austrian Poland (including Poland's second city, Cracow) in exchange. The Kaiser was noncommittal. Throughout the remainder of Holy Week, after returning to Vienna, Charles worked on a formal document which would set before the Kaiser in the starkest terms the absolute necessity of peace. When delivered the next week it bore Czernin's signature, but its principal author was Charles.

> It is absolutely plain that our military strength is nearing its end. . . . I need refer only to the shortage of raw materials for munitions production; our completely exhausted manpower reserves; and, above all, the mood of deadening desperation which undernourishment produces among all sections of the people. . . . *We must make an end at any price by the late summer or autumn of 1917.* . . . (67)

> The amazing facility with which the strongest monarchy in the world [Russia] was overthrown may well cause us anxiety and call to mind the saying: *Exemplae trahunt.* Let it not be said that in Germany or Austro-Hungary the conditions are different. Let it not be argued that the deep-rooted monarchist feelings in both Berlin and Vienna rule out the possibility of such a development. It is without example and without precedent. The world is no longer what it was three years ago and it would be vain to seek a historical parallel for the happenings which have now become daily occurrences.(68)

This was no mere theoretical observation on current events and prospects, nor was it only a generalized warning of the dangers of revolution in Germany and Austria if the war continued indefinitely. It had a much more specific referent. For Charles had learned, either just before or during his conference with Kaiser Wilhelm April 3, of a plan carefully developed by the German High Command in conjuction with the Foreign Office: to use revolution as a weapon, like poison gas and the stalking submarine, by sending Lenin and a contingent of his Bolsheviks from the haven in Switzerland to Russia by sealed railway car in the expectation that they would help knock Russia out of the war. The original plan called for the trip to be made across Austrian territory. At the Homburg conference, Charles made known to Wilhelm personally his total opposition to this plan, which he later conveyed officially and explicitly to the German government. Zita has reported his grounds for opposition as follows:

> First, that this was an unfair and irresponsible thing to do to the Russian people. Second, that the more chaos was caused in Russia the more difficult it would be to find anyone to talk peace

with. And third, that once Communism got established in Russia, it wouldn't stop there but would spread and both Germany and Austro-Hungary could become engulfed. Evil, he was convinced, could only breed evil.(69)

As for the train carrying Lenin and his cohorts crossing Austrian territory, Charles said: Never.

The German government routed it through Germany to Sweden instead.

After a farewell lunch at Zurich's Hotel Zahringer Hof, Lenin set out with a party of 32 adults and four children from Zurich's huge railroad station for the first leg of the journey—probably the most important train trip in the history of the world. At least 25 of his group were Bolsheviks, including seven women. They carried baskets and string bags. Lenin wore a derby hat, a heavy coat, and thick hobnailed boots, and carried an umbrella. On the station platform, Marxist and anti-German demonstrators clashed; several of the Bolsheviks had to fight their way onto the train, Lenin using the handle of his umbrella to good effect as a club. Siegfried Bloch, a Swiss Marxist, ran up to Lenin to shake his hand in farewell, saying: "I hope to see you soon back among us, comrade."

"If we come back soon it won't be a good sign for the revolution," Lenin replied in his abrupt way.(70) He threw an intruder off the train, settled down in a compartment with Krupskaya, took out his omnipresent notebook, and began to write. He was never to see Switzerland again.

The train, typically Swiss, pulled out despite all the commotion exactly on time, at 3:10 p.m. April 9. It was Easter Monday.

After half an hour's delay at the frontier, the train passed into Germany. Lenin wrote incessantly. Krupskaya remembered seeing only old men and women in the villages; all the youth had been swept up by the war. The country was starving. Security on the train, provided by German soldier-guards, was tight: only Fritz Platten, a Swiss Marxist who had helped arrange the trip with the German authorities, was permitted off the train periodically to buy newspapers and beer. No words were exchanged between the party of Russians and any Germans except the soldier-guards. The journey ended three days later at the Baltic port of Sassnitz, where the Bolsheviks were locked in hotel rooms for the night.

The next morning they took the ferry for Sweden. The sea was rough. Lenin went up to the bridge with the captain. He was there when the message arrived from his contact in Sweden, Ganetsky, to confirm that he was on the boat. The ferry landed at dusk. Robert Payne memorably describes the scene:

> One by one they came down the gangplank, gray with fatigue and green with seasickness, carrying their baskets and string parcels, while the children wept and their mothers tried to comfort them; and no one seeing that straggling crowd on the wharf in the gray light of a Baltic evening would have guessed they were conquerors who would soon take Russia by storm.(71)

It was April 13, Good Friday in Russia. All over that great war-stricken land the faithful gathered in the churches to commemorate the crucifixion of the Son of God, the Savior of mankind—the day when they clubbed Him, whipped Him, crowned Him with thorns, hammered the nails into His hands and His feet, opened His side with a lance, and saw Him put away in a closely guarded tomb.

Sleepless, tireless, Lenin stayed up almost all night on the train from Malmo to Stockhom, spent the day Saturday the 14th in a round of conferences and shopping (books and clothes) in Stockholm, and left for Finland on the evening train, without staying a single night in the Swedish capital. On Sunday the 15th, the Russian Easter morning, he reached the frontier of Finland, then still ruled by Russia, where he was officially readmitted to the country of his birth. At eleven o'clock Sunday night he arrived at Belo-Ostrov on the Finnish-Russian border, where he was enthusiastically greeted by about 100 Bolsheviks from Petrograd. Lenin, exiled for nearly ten years, had become a legend—the "mountain eagle of the revolution," the man of iron will far away, the relentless man who never faltered, never slackened, always knew exactly where he was going. Already, in his "letters from afar," sent from Switzerland to Russia, he had denounced the Provisional Government in the most scathing terms. His attitude

toward it had been summed up in a telegram to Marxists in
Sweden March 19:

> Our tactic: absolute distrust, no support for the new
> government, above all we are suspicious of Kerensky, the
> proletariat is the sole guarantee, immediate election of the
> Petrograd Duma, no reconciliation with other parties.(72)

"Absolute distrust. . .No reconciliation." That was Lenin, to the
core.

At eleven o'clock in the evening of April 16, the Russian Easter
Monday, a national holiday, Lenin arrived at the Finland station in
Petrograd. The Bolsheviks had prepared a tremendous welcome.
The station blazed with red banners. There were triumphal arches
decorated with red ribbons and revolutionary slogans. Searchlights from the Peter and Paul Fortress nearby played on the
station square, which was filled with workers carrying banners and
torches. On the platform at which Lenin's train arrived were large
detachments of soldiers, sailors, and "Red Guard" militia, and a
band playing the Marseillaise. Lenin reviewed the sailors, very
much as though he were already their commander; then he was
taken to the former imperial waiting room in the station, carrying a
lush bouquet of red roses presented by his great admirer
Alexandra Kollontai. It jarred harshly with his cold, domineering
manner. The Petrograd Soviet had designated Nikolai Chkeidze, a
leading Menshevik Marxist and long-time opponent of Lenin, to
deliver a welcome which quickly became a warning.

> The principal task of the revolutionary democracy at present is to
> defend our revolution from every kind of attack both from within
> and from without. We believe that what is needed is not disunity
> but the closing of the ranks of the entire democracy. We hope
> you will pursue these aims together with us.(73)

Chkeidze knew Lenin all too well. All present noted his gloom, as
he spoke; some suspected his fear.

In his "reply," Lenin simply ignored Chkeidze's existence.

> Dear comrades, soldiers, sailors and workers! I am happy to
> greet in your persons the victorious Russian revolution! I greet
> you as the vanguard of the world proletarian army. The
> predatory imperialist war is the beginning of a civil war all over
> Europe. . . . Any day now we shall see the collapse of European

imperialism. The Russian revolution you have made has
prepared the way and opened a new epoch. Long live the world
socialist revolution!(74)

The soldiers and sailors then rushed into the waiting room and
carried Lenin on their shoulders out to the station square with its
cheering masses, lifting him up to the turret of an armored car so
that he might speak to them, as from a pulpit. He stood on the
turret, illuminated in sweeps by the searchlights, stamping his
feet, clenching his fists, and shouting his slogans which the crowd
echoed back. They sensed the elemental force of the man, his
gigantic capacity for leadership; in the disturbed, distorted
atmosphere of a revolution just one month old, made in despair
without plan or clear purpose, when so much that was familiar and
solid in their city and in their land had already dissolved, no
doctrine could seem too wild, no call to action too strident, no
denunciation too harsh.

Lenin knew it. No man in all history has known better how to
take the fullest advantage of fundamental political opportunity. He
did not waste an hour or a minute. His armored car led a
procession of vehicles from the Finland station to the nearby
Kshesinskaya Palace which the Bolsheviks had commandeered; at
several cross streets, Lenin stopped the car and gave a short
speech from the turret. Only snatches from those speeches were
remembered and recorded.

> Capitalist robbers . . . the destruction of the people of Europe for
> the sake of the profits of a handful of exploiters . . . The defense
> of the fatherland means the defense of one gang of capitalists
> from another gang!(75)

At the palace, from one o'clock to three o'clock Tuesday
morning the 17th, Lenin spoke to the Bolshevik leaders. "He kept
hammering, hammering, hammering, and at last he made them
his captives," said the Bolshevik journalist Sukhanov later, having
been the only person present who was not a senior party leader.
When it was over, he said, "I felt as though I had been beaten
about the head with flails." All power to the Soviets! Down with
the Provisional Government! No concessions to those who wanted
to carry on the war! "We don't need any parliamentary republic!
We don't need any bourgeois democracy!" Confiscate all property

in land! Nationalize all the banks! Abolish the army, the bureaucracy, the police! And finally, since "the majority of the Social Democrats [Marxists] all over the world have betrayed socialism and gone over to the side of the government," "in my own name I propose that the name of the party be changed to the Communist Party." "Have the will to build a new party!"(76)

These, Lenin's extraordinary, overwhelming "April Theses," were elaborated and officially presented to a meeting of all the Bolshevik delegates to the All-Russian Conference of Soviets of Workers' and Soldiers' Deputies at the Tauride Palace the next morning, and then published April 20 in *Pravda*, the Bolshevik daily newspapter. They were too much even for the Bolsheviks, at first. One of their most respected leaders, Kamenev, denounced them in *Pravda* the following day as premature and impractical at best. Lenin was contemptuous of such opposition and angry because it was widespread, even in his own party. By sheer force of will, he broke most of his opponents in face-to-face encounters. In the process, just before the end of April, he found one man, cold, hard, almost emotionless, untroubled by scruples of any kind, whom he was sure he could use. Up to this point this man had been, in Sukhanov's words, only "a gray blur" behind the scenes. (77) In 1915 Lenin had had to ask a friend to recall for him his name. But now Lenin went up to Joseph Djugashvili (party names Koba and Stalin), clapped him on the shoulder, and congratulated him for being a man of action instead of an "intellectual nincompoop" like so many others in the party. Lenin said to Stalin:

> Come, we two shall form an alliance. The Provisional Government must be overthrown, and we shall overthrow it when the masses are with us! I guarantee they will be with us very soon, because we shall promise them everything they can demand from a victorious revolution. Will you join me?(78)

Thus did Lenin make his protege the man who was to be, in all probability, his murderer; the man of whom Robert Payne says:

> This small, brooding, pock-marked man with a crooked arm, black teeth and yellow eyes, was the greatest tyrant of his time, and perhaps of all time.(79)

******

The day Lenin arrived at the Finland station was the day General Nivelle's offensive began on the Western front. For an assault out of the trenches there to have the slightest chance of success, the weather had to be good; otherwise any attack would quickly bog down in omnipresent mud. On April 15, the day before Nivelle's attack, it began to rain heavily. In the evening the rain turned to sleet. By the dawn of April 16, when the assault was scheduled to jump off, the battlefield was already a half-frozen quagmire, the worst possible conditions.

Nivelle nevertheless ordered the attack to proceed in full force, with no less than 31 divisions engaged at the outset, and additional units being brought up from the rear and fed into the fighting every fifteen minutes throughout the day.

In the course of the morning the sleet became mixed with snow, the combination falling so heavily that the French gunners could not see the battle area at all. They began dropping their barrages on their own men. By mid-afternoon a German counterattack on the confused, battered mass of French troops bunched near their own trenches completed the disaster. The medical service was overwhelmed. All night the wounded were dying in the freezing mud, calling piteously for help that never came.

On that one day, April 16, 1917, the day of "the tragedy of Chemin des Dames,"(80) the French army suffered *ninety thousand casualties*—to gain, at a few points, a few hundred yards.

Even yet the hallucinated Nivelle would not stop, would not admit error or failure. For the rest of the month French attacks continued in the same area, though on a smaller and smaller scale. The government could not decide whether or when to relieve Nivelle. Haig, perhaps recognizing a kindred spirit, urged that he be retained. There were scattered, disturbing incidents in the army. Soldiers of the First Colonial Infantry Division, being withdrawn from the front, screamed from their trucks as they passed soldiers going up to the front: "Long live peace! We're through with killing!"(81) On April 29 the Second Battalion of the 18th Infantry Regiment was ordered back to the front after having lost two-thirds of its men in the assault of April 16. The battalion refused to march.

This first of the French army mutinies lasted only a few hours. The battalion was quickly forced back to obedience, and four soldiers thought to be ringleaders of the mutiny were shot. But the warning was vivid and unmistakable. There would be more mutinies soon.

* * * * * *

On April 19 Prime Minister David Lloyd George of England and French Premier Alexandre Ribot met in a railway carriage at a little town in the French Alps with Baron Sidney Sonnino, the Italian Foreign Minister, to discuss the terms of a separate peace with Austria. Prince Sixtus, meeting with Lloyd George in Paris on his way to this conference, had obtained from him a promise not to mention to Sonnino Charles' letter, fearing for his brother-in-law's life should the full contents of the letter become known to the Germans. But even if he had known the source of the Austrian peace proposals put before him by Lloyd George, it seems most unlikely that Sonnino would have been inclined to accept them. For he was the architect of the secret treaty of 1915 by which Great Britain and France promised Italy virtually the whole coastline of the Austrian Empire and half of its heartland province, the Tyrol—areas which had been Austrian for 150 years or more, and which the Italian army had conspicuously failed to conquer even in the smallest part. Charles would never give them all up, though for peace he might relinquish some small portions. But Sonnino demanded them all, and would consider no peace without them. Regarding themselves as bound by the secret treaty and therefore unable to negotiate further without Italy, Lloyd George and Ribot had to inform Sixtus they were at an impasse. He would have to get in touch with Charles and give him the bad news.

So the war and the slaughter, the "living hell of the trenches," must go on—and with it, the Communist revolution in Russia. Men had failed—even a man, Charles, who may well have been a saint. In the end the troops from America would probably bring a barren victory out of it all. But—as Woodrow Wilson had wondered aloud to Frank Cobb on the eve of the U.S. declaration of war—what would then be left to win?

In the terrible words of Paul Nash, describing the Western front:

> No pen or drawing can convey this country—the normal setting of the battles taking place day and night, month after month. Evil and the incarnate fiend alone can be master of this war, and no glimmer of God's hand is seen anywhere. Sunset and sunrise are blasphemous, they are mockeries to man, only the black rain out of the bruised and swollen clouds all through the bitter black of night is fit atmosphere in such a land. The rain drives on, the stinking mud becomes evilly yellow, the shell-holes fill up with green-white water, the roads and tracks are covered in inches of slime, the black dying trees ooze and sweat and the shells never cease. They alone plunge overhead, tearing away the rotting tree stumps . . . annihilating, maiming, maddening, they plunge into the grave which is this land; one huge grave, and cast upon it the poor dead. It is unspeakable, godless, hopeless.(82)

May 1917

But God made the world and He will not leave it, though He hang dead upon its cross when the darkness falls, as on that day at the Place of the Skull in Jerusalem almost nineteen hundred years before the First World War.

Watch for the candle in the night—to become a sun dancing in the sky.

God has a vicar upon the earth. In these years of horror he was a frail wisp of a man, who never in his life would have been fit to charge a machine gun; but Pope Benedict XV's heart and mind and soul were not weak, only his body. Like the prophet Isaiah, he "cried out without ceasing." In his first statement as Pope, on September 8, 1914, he mourned the bloodshed and pleaded for a quick end to the war just begun—gently, lovingly, yet with a vein of iron, a reminder that all men, including rulers, will ultimately face a Judge untouchable by propaganda or force: "the rulers of the peoples," Pope Benedict XV said, should "be satisfied with the ruin already wrought."(83)

In his first encyclical, *Ad Beatissimi*, issued November 1, 1914, he asked sadly, surveying the Christian peoples whom God had entrusted to his spiritual care: "Who could realize that they are brethren, children of the same Father in Heaven?"(84) The encyclical closed with a call for prayer to Christ, the giver of peace, and to the Blessed Virgin Mary, "who bore the Prince of Peace."

Constantly pressured to condemn one side or the other, Pope Benedict XV would condemn nothing and no one but the war itself—that "unparalleled scourge," that "carnage which is without example," that "monstrous spectacle," that "horrible plague" (to select only a few of his epithets for it).(85) On

82

Christmas Eve 1914, in an unforgettable allocution to the cardinals, bishops, and other leaders of the Church in Rome, he rose to oratorical heights no one had ever suspected he could touch:

> May the fraticidal weapons fall to the ground! Already the are too bloodstained; let them at last fall! And may the hands of those who have had to wield them return to the labors of industry and commerce, to the works of civilization and peace.(86)

For Holy Week of 1915 he launched a prayer campaign for peace throughout Europe, composing and sending out to all the warring nations a passionate appeal to the King of Kings:

> In this hour made terrible with burning hate, with bloodshed and with slaughter, once more may Thy divine Heart be moved to pity. Pity the countless mothers in anguish for the fate of their sons; pity the numberless families now bereaved of their fathers; pity Europe over which broods such havoc and disaster. Do Thou inspire rulers and peoples with counsels of meekness, do Thou heal the discords that tear the nations asunder; Thou Who didst shed They Precious Blood that they might live as brothers, bring men together once more in loving harmony. And as once before to the cry of the Apostle Peter: *Save us, Lord, we perish*, Thou didst answer with words of mercy and didst still the raging waves, so now deign to hear our trustful prayer, and give back to the world peace and tranquillity.
>
> And do thou, O most holy Virgin, as in other times of sore distress, be now our help, our protection and our safeguard.(87)

This prayer was condemned by the young Benito Mussolini, seized as subversive by the French police, and carefully "explained" by the Cardinal Archbishop of Paris in a sermon at the Church of the Sacred Heart on Montmartre as really being a call for "a victorious peace" for France. Meanwhile the Germans thought they has reached a height of magnanimity by allowing captured French and Belgian priests to be granted, as prisoners, the status of officers rather than of enlisted men.

A Pope may not despair, and Benedict XV never did. But by 1916 he was reaching far beyond this world in his quest for peace. On July 30—about the time the Angel of Peace came to the children of Fatima, and the second anniversary of the war—he called together five thousand child communicants for a special blessing at the Vatican and delivered to them a homily and an appeal unique in the 2000-year history of the Papacy:

> In order that the record of this moment may remain graven on
> your minds all your lives and that you may ever have to
> remember what you heard at this fatal time from the very lips of
> Christ's Vicar, learn from Us also, my children, how for two long
> years men who were once innocent and affectionate like you, and
> are so no longer, have been tearing and killing each other.
> . . . You are taking part in the most fearful expiation that God, in
> His hidden and infinite design, ever wrought by the hands of
> guilty society. . . . Therefore We have resolved to betake
> Ourself, as to a last plank in shipwreck, to invoking the help of
> God through the all-powerful means of your innocence. . . .
> Stretch out a hand then, dear and all powerful children, to the
> Vicar of Christ and strengthen his unceasing desires with you
> precious prayers. Will your parents, your brothers, all the older
> members of your families follow in your humble footsteps?
> . . . You know what We desire. We desire that mankind may
> cease from hatred and slaughter, and after having been so
> wickedly fellows of Cain may become instead fellows of Abel by
> the works of grace, labor and pardon. . . . May God, who spared
> from death the sons of the Hebrews through the blood which
> gleamed red as a sign on the doors of their houses, spare you and
> your household and the entire world every further shedding of
> blood by the merits of that infinitely precious stream which
> bathed the cross of the Divine Son and which today, after the
> mystic banquet, gleams red on your lips, symbol once again of
> the Redemption and of the pardon which Jesus alone can
> give.(88)

To no avail. . .in human terms, to no avail. The war went on:
the Somme, Verdun, the Nivelle offensive, unrestricted submarine
warfare, the revolution in Russia. It was May, sweet spring, the
season of the Risen Christ; but Europe was more than ever the
antechamber of Hell.

On May 5 Pope Benedict XV, in a letter to Cardinal Gasparri,
his secretary of state, recalled his pleas for peace during 1915:

> Our earnestly pleading voice, invoking the end of the vast
> conflict, the suicide of civilized Europe, was then and has
> remained ever since unheard. Indeed, it seemed that the dark
> tide of hatred grew higher and wider among the belligerent
> nations, and drew other countries into its frightful sweep,
> multiplying ruin and massacre. Nevertheless Our confidence was
> not lessened. . . . Since all graces which the Author of all good

deigns to grant to the poor children of Adam, by a loving design
of His Divine Providence are dispensed through the hands of the
most holy Virgin, we wish that the petition of her most afflicted
children, more than ever in this terrible hour, may turn with
lively confidence to the august Mother of God.(89)

He directed that the invocation "Queen of peace, pray for us," be
added permanently to the Litany of Loreto; and then, fixing his
soul's gaze upon her who had borne God in her womb and in her
arms in Bethlehem, the loving mother of all Christians as she is the
loving Mother of God, he made his ultimate appeal:

> To Mary, then, who is the Mother of Mercy and omnipotent by
> grace, let loving and devout appeal go up from every corner of
> the earth—from noble temples and tiniest chapels, from royal
> palaces and mansions of the rich as from the poorest hut—from
> every place wherein a faithful soul finds shelter—from
> blood-drenched plains and seas. Let it bear to her the anguished
> cry of mothers and wives, the wailing of innocent little ones, the
> sighs of every generous heart: that her most tender and benign
> solicitude may be moved and the peace we ask for be obtained
> for our agitated world.(90)

Eight days later, Sunday, May 13, 1917, she came herself, in
person.

It was a glorious spring day in the heart of Portugal. Lucia and
Jacinta and Francisco, having been to Mass at the little parish
church at Fatima, had taken their sheep to pasture in the grassy
depression among the hills called the Cova da Iria. As they played
happily, there came out of the cloudless, deep blue sky a brilliant
flash of light—and then, in a few minutes, another. There was no
thunder, only the flashes. The children, frightened, were running
away, when they stopped short upon seeing before them, atop a
small evergreen tree about three feet tall, a ball of light, within
which stood a Lady clad in a white which Lucia later described as
"more brilliant than the sun dispensing light, clearer and more
intense than a crystal cup full of crystalline water penetrated by
the rays of the most glaring sun." Her face too was bathed in
dazzling light. It was "not sad, not happy, but serious." Her
hands were joined in prayer; a rosary was suspended from her
right hand. The children where within two yards of her.

"Don't be afraid," she said. "I won't hurt you." Her voice was

low, musical, gentle. They would never forget the lovely sound of
it.

"Where does Your Excellency come from?" asked Lucia,
greatly daring.

"I am from Heaven."

"And what is it you want of me?"

"I come to ask you to come here for six months in succession,
on the thirteenth day at the same hour. Then I will tell you who I
am, and what I want."(91)

She promised all three of them that they would go to Heaven;
but then she asked them:

> "Do you wish to offer yourselves to God, to endure all the
> suffering that He may please to send you, as an act of reparation
> for the sins by which He is offended, and to ask for the
> conversion of sinners?"
>
> "Yes, we do."
>
> "Then you will have much to suffer. But the grace of God will
> be your comfort."(92)

She opened her hands. The radiance grew, seeming to
penetrate their very souls, "making us see ourselves in God more
clearly in that light than in the best of mirrors," as Lucia described
it later.

So far, everything the Lady said had concerned the children
personally—their calling, their salvation. Now, in her last words to
them this day, the Mother of God addressed the immense crisis
that had brought her from Heaven: "Say the Rosary every day, to
obtain peace for the world, and the end of the war."(93)

Rising from the top of the little tree, she slipped away into the
sky toward the east, where the sun comes up.

The three children went home transfigured with joy. Jacinta
simply could not keep the secret. She told her mother, and then
her father, who closely questioned her and Francisco. Manuel
Pedro Marto was not a man given to enthusiasm. He was a slow,
careful countryman, firmly erect, quietly decisive, a man with a
solidly unshakeable grip on reality, one of the often nameless
millions who have borne the world's empires and armies and
nobilities and cities on their strong backs and shoulders, for ten
thousand years. He had never learned to read or write. But like

most of his kind in lands to which the good news of Christ has come, Manuel Pedro Marto was a believer—a believer, but no fanatic.

After considering all he had heard from his children, he said:

> From the beginning of the world Our Lady has appeared many times in various ways. If the world is wicked, it would be much more so but for many such happenings. The power of God is great. We don't know what this is, but it will turn out to be something.(94)

Lucia's parents refused to believe her at all, and scolded and threatened her, trying to persuade her to give up her story. She held serenely firm. The three children offered up to Christ their sufferings through the ridicule of friends and adults; they went without lunch, even without water, each day they were out with the sheep, to suffer in reparation for sin as the Lady had asked. One day two priests visited Lucia; they asked her to pray for the Pope, the Vicar of Christ, the visible head of the Church, who was suffering very much and needed their prayers. (Had they read, or heard of, his homily to the child communicants the preceding summer in Rome?) Every day after that the children added three Hail Marys for Benedict XV to their Rosary for peace which the Lady had asked them to pray. And they waited for June 13, when she would come back again.

* * * * * *

For the warring powers of Europe May was a pause, a lull, a calm between storms. The horror and the killing continued on the Western front, but for the moment at a reduced level, since most of the French army would no longer fight offensively; on May 15 Nivelle was finally replaced by Marshal Petain, who had commanded at Verdun. In Russia the influence of the Communists steadily grew, as Trotsky returned with great fanfare and joined Lenin, and Communist agitation spread among the soldiers of an army now at least as mutinous as the French. Kerensky's Provisional Government remained more or less in control; but at a meeting of increasingly desperate officers in Mogilev May 20 General Mikhail Alexeyev, commander-in-chief of the Russian armies, warned starkly: "Russia is dying. She stands on the edge of an abyss."(95) (Two weeks later the Kerensky government dismissed Alexeyev because he did not think a new Russian offensive practicable in the view of the collapse of military discipline.) Sinkings of merchant ships by German submarines in British waters reached a peak and began to decline as, at the strong urging of U.S. Admiral William S. Sims, the convoy system was introduced to protect them. The German socialist leader Scheidemann called for peace without annexations or indemnities, and was widely and furiously denounced throughout Germany for doing so. Britian's General Haig, aware of the danger of a complete collapse of the French army due to the rapid spread of mutiny from the traumatic effects of the Nivelle disaster, was preparing an offensive on his main front in Flanders to draw German attention away from the French lines—another offensive of the same old frontal, bloody, futile kind.

As for the peace initiative of Emperor Charles through Prince Sixtus, attempts to revive it made little progress. Through Sixtus, Charles offered to give up the Italian-speaking portion of the South Tyrol (the Trentino) if some compensating territory were supplied to Austria; but Sonnino of Italy would not budge, and Lloyd George's effort to go over his head to the King of Italy came to nothing. By the latter part of May the French government had lost interest in the negotiations. By some perversion of the reasoning faculty, Premier Ribot and Foreign Minister Cambon had convinced themselves that it was better to have Italy in the war fighting Austria than to have both Austria and Italy out of war fighting nobody, with Germany totally isolated. Ribot wrote the epitaph of the noblest and most disinterested peace offer by any belligerent in the whole course of this war, in an ugly, snarling speech in the French Chamber of Deputies May 22, which was rapturously received by his fellow belligerents in France and elsewhere:

> They [the Central Powers] will come to us asking for peace, not as they come today, hypocritically through indirect and ambiguous channels, but openly and honorably; and we will make peace on conditions worthy of France, of France in the past

and of our Frace today. If they do not ask us for peace, we shall
find out the way to enforce it on them. (loud applause from all
parts)(96)

For nearly three years Pope Benedict XV had waited in vain for
the belligerents to listen to prayers and pleas and reason, and
make peace themselves, but they would not; they were still only
talking about how to "enforce it on" their enemies. Whether or
how much he knew of Charles' peace initiative through
Prince Sixtus had never been made clear. Knowing or sensing the
likely fate of any such endeavor as Charles had made, even after
all the long futility and horror of the war, the Pope was now
prepared to advance specific proposals himself. On the very day
the Blessed Virgin Mary came to the children in the Cova da Iria, a
young Vatican diplomat named Eugenio Pacelli (one day to be
Pope Pius XII) was consecrated archbishop in the Sistine Chapel,
under the world-famous ceiling frescoes of Michelangelo, where
the College of Cardinals meets to elect Popes. This rapid and high
elevation in clerical rank was to enable him to go with suitable
dignity to all-Catholic Bavaria as Papal nuncio. From there he
would approach the German government with a direct Papal peace
offer.

June 1917

On the thirteenth of June, while the relative lull in the war still continued, the Lady came back to the Cova da Iria.

This time some fifty people were there with the children, for word of what they had seen had spread, and some believed them. Lucia's parents still did not believe her, and Jacinta's and Francisco's still had sufficient doubt so that they arranged to be away on the appointed day. Those present said five decades of the Rosary with the three children. Then the children saw her come, in the same way and to the same place as on May 13, atop the little three-foot evergreen tree.

No one else saw her. But Maria Carreira, a quietly honest eyewitness, has reported hearing a faint sound, "like the buzzing of a bee," from the top of the little tree when Lucia heard the Lady speaking to her; others noticed a brief dimming of the sun's light and a bending of the branches and leaves of the tree. As on May 13, though Francisco saw her, he did not hear her words.

The Lady said to Lucia:

"I want you to come here on the thirteenth day of the coming month, to recite five decades of the Rosary every day, and to learn to read."

She repeated her assurance of May that Jacinta and Francisco would soon be with her in Heaven, but that Lucia would remain on earth for a long time, since "Jesus wishes to make use of you to have me acknowledge and loved. . .to establish in the world the devotion to my Immaculate Heart."

Lucia protested that she did not want to remain alone. The Lady told her she would not be alone.

"Do you suffer a great deal? Don't be discouraged. I will never forsake you. My Immaculate Heart will be your refuge and the road that will conduct you to God.''(97)

She told them a secret, which has never been revealed; then she showed them a vision of her Immaculate Heart, encircled by piercing thorns representing the sins that wounded it; and she departed into the east as before. The upper leaves of the little tree remained for several hours stretched and bending toward the east.

The next day Lucia, Jacinta and Francisco were closely questioned by Father Manuel Ferreira, the parish priest at Fatima. He concluded that they were telling the truth about what they had seen, but brought up for the first time the possibility that the visions were deceptions of the Devil, an idea the children indignantly rejected. In the end, Father Ferreira said he simply could not make up his mind about what they had seen; but he did believe they had seen something.

* * * * * *

In France the army mutinies, after reaching a high point of extent and danger early in the month but without ever quite becoming a general, concerted outbreak, were gradually being brought under control by the conciliatory measures of Marshal Petain in dealing somewhat more considerately with the troops, particularly regarding quarters and leave policy. During the first week of June, however, Petain said he had only two wholly reliable divisions between the front and Paris. Obviously it would be folly to talk of any new French offensive soon.

Haig stepped in to provide a British offensive instead.

For three decisive days—June 19, 20, and 21—in a series of conferences, Lloyd George and four of his chief ministers who, with him, made up the British Committee on War Policy, met with Haig and the Chief of Staff, Marshal Robertson. It was Nivelle revisited. Lloyd George has described Haig's briefing as follows:

> When Sir Douglas Haig explained the projects to the civilians, he spread on a table or desk a large map and made a dramatic use of both his hands to demonstrate how he proposed to sweep up the enemy—first the right hand brushing along the surface

irresistibly, and then came the left, his outer finger ultimately touching the German frontier with the nail across.(98)

The French would aid in the assault, Haig asserted, despite their demoralized condition. The Germans "realize that they are beaten"; American observers had reported they "no longer present a smart appearance."(99) He doubted the Germans had artillery superiority as the British War Office believed; even if they did have it, this could be disregarded because their fire was inaccurate. Passchendaele ridge, the first objective, would be quickly seized. This would be followed in a short time by the capture of the entire Belgian coast, now all in German hands.

The entire Belgian coast! A silence fell. No one could think of what to say to that. It would require an advance of no less than forty miles, across dead-flat terrain, at or below sea level, ideal for the machine gun, with bottomless mud when it rained (as it frequently did), smashing through German defenses dug, protected, and perfected during three years of a war in which, the year before, an advance of just eight miles in more favorable terrain near the Somme had cost six hundred thousand Allied casualties when it finally ground to a halt. Haig proposed to go five times as far. Did he intend to expend three million men?

It was madness. Once again, as in the last April days before Nivelle sacrificed ninety thousand men on the altar of his pride in the first day of his foredoomed offensive, no one had the courage to say it to Haig's face, or Robertson's. The two men coldly rejected every argument and every warning of the consequences of their plan which they received during the three days of conferences, and virtually dared Lloyd George to stop them. He did not dare. As he said later:

> Profound though my own apprehensions of failure were, I was a layman and in matters of military strategy I did not possess the knowledge and training that would justify me in overriding soldiers of such standing and experience. Accordingly, the soldiers had their way. And it is one of the bitter ironies of war that I, who have been ruthlessly assailed in books, in the press and in speeches for "interfering with the soldiers" should carry with me as my most painful regret the memory that on this issue I did *not* justify that charge.(100)

Still, he did make Haig and Robertson promise "that if the progress they made with the operation did not realize the expectations they had formed, it should be called off."(101)

The promise was not kept.

* * * * * *

On June 26 Archbishop Pacelli presented his credentials in Berlin as Papal nuncio and met with Chancellor Bethmann-Hollweg, who was now under enormous pressure from the advocates of war to the finish at any cost, in the military and elsewhere, to reject out of hand any serious negotiations for peace and to refuse to renounce imperialist war aims. The severity of the pressure may be gauged by Bethmann-Hollweg's statement in May of his wish that he were in the trenches rather than in the Imperial Chancellery, because in the trenches his agony might be quickly ended by an enemy bullet. In this state of near despair Bethmann-Hollweg, though a Protestant and reputedly anti-Catholic, welcomed Pacelli and in his first response to the Papal peace offer, agreed to the full restoration of Belgium, to arms limitation and court arbitration of international disputes, and even to opening negotiations without excluding in advance the return of any part of Alsace-Lorraine to France.

These were the most substantial and specific concessions the German government had offered since the war began—made against the background of a furious clamor by the militarists to the Kaiser for Bethmann-Hollweg's immediate dismissal from office. The next day, June 27, two leading German socialists, Scheidemann and David, just returned from an international socialist conference in Stockholm where they had found not the slightest sign of support for war concessions from their socialist "comrades" in the Entente nations, told Bethmann-Hollweg bluntly that Germany must make at once a firm public commitment to peace without annexations or indemnities. Bethmann-Hollweg replied that personally he agreed with them, but was no longer sure of his ability to gain approval for such a declaration from the Kaiser, now so much influenced by his generals, especially

Ludendorff.

On June 29 Bethmann-Hollweg made his effort to persuade the Kaiser, who in turn tried to persuade the generals. Hindenburg was somewhat receptive, but Ludendorff remained immovable. On his massive monocled figure the proposal shipwrecked, as the Charles-Sixtus peace initiative had shipwrecked on Sonnino of Italy.

That same day the Kaiser received Pacelli, who gave him Pope Benedict XV's personal, handwritten letter pleading with Wilhelm to make a greater effort for peace. For a time the two men fenced, with the Kaiser claiming that the Pope should have responded to his own "peace note" of December 12, 1916 (which had not made a single offer or concession, but simply—though very grandiloquently—expressed willingness to begin negotiations) and Pacelli pointing out that this "proposal" had provided nothing concrete for the Pope to respond to. The full restoration of Belgium, Pacelli stated quietly but firmly, was absolutely indispensable to peace. He made some mention of harsh German measures in Belgium, such as the deportation of Belgian workers to Germany.

The Kaiser—who, despite his caricatures, was far from a totally evil man—had the grace to admit that the deportations might have been wrong. But then he began to work himself up into a temper, a besetting vice of his especially when he was under the kind of pressure Bethmann-Hollweg and Ludendorff had been exerting on him that day from opposite sides. Why didn't the Pope denounce Entente atrocities? Since he claimed infallibility, all the Catholics in the Entente nations would have to listen to him! Finally, carried away by temper, the Kaiser had the appalling effrontery to suggest that the Pope "edify" the world by dying as a martyr to stop the war.

Pacelli, in reply, could have spoken of white martyrdom. But we do not know if he thought that remark worthy of any reply at all.

Kaiser Wilhelm II was no longer, if indeed he had ever really been, master in his own house. Nor was Bethmann-Hollweg; his long, soul-wracking tenure of office, which had begun in those almost unimaginably distant, halcyon days before the war, had just two weeks left to run. Then General Erich von Ludendorff, that incarnation of the Prussian militarist, a prime mover of the plan to send Lenin to Russia, later to be the only significant supporter of Adolf Hitler in his first bid for power in Munich—the "beer hall *putsch*"—would become the effective ruler of Germany.

The next day—the last day of June—Pacelli was in Austria, where Charles assured him that he was indeed prepared to discuss and negotiate the cession of the Italian-speaking parts of the South Tyrol to Italy, in return for peace.

The Mother of God had said, when first she came in May: "Say the Rosary every day, to obtain peace for the world, and the end of the war."

July 1917

The thirteenth of July was the day when Bethmann-Hollweg was finally forced to resign as Chancellor of the German Empire, leaving the dominant policy-making role in Germany to Ludendorff, who picked the obscure bureaucrat Georg Michaelis as the next Chancellor. Meanwhile General Haig was pressing forward toward his Passchendaele offensive in Flanders, scheduled to begin before the end of the month. The war would go on, unchanged.

On the thirteenth of July the Mother of God appeared for the third time to Lucia and Jacinta and Francisco at the Cova da Iria.

Lucia, under great pressure from her mother, almost did not go this time; at the last moment Jacinta persuaded her. When the three children arrived, they found at least two thousand people waiting. This time their parents were present also. The two mothers were distraught—Lucia's unbelieving and hostile, Jacinta's and Francisco's deeply doubtful. But Manuel Pedro Marto was increasingly sure of the truth of what his son and daughter had seen. He was there to protect them, and Lucia. He never took his eyes off them.

He saw Lucia go pale, even before she cried out that Our Lady was coming. The he saw "something like a small cloud" come down upon the little tree in the Cova; the hot July sunlight dimmed, a cool breeze sprang up, and he heard a sound which he described, in his homely way, as "like a horse-fly in an empty water-pot."(102)

The Blessed Virgin Mary, who as a girl in Nazareth had known both flies and pots, would not have objected to the description; for the words spoken in her low, gentle, musical voice were for the children alone—the rest would hear only a sound that corresponded to something in their experience, without being intelligible as words.

Mary asked the children to come again on the thirteenth of the next month and to continue saying five decades of the Rosary every day for peace. She promised a miracle in October to convince the people that she was real. She spoke again of propagating devotion to her Immaculate Heart, for the conversion of sinners and in reparation for sin. To show the children the full evil and consequences of great sin, so that they would understand the profound need for such conversion and reparation, she showed them a vision of Hell and its denizens, "a sea of fire, and plunged in this fire the demons and the souls, as if they were red-hot coals."

Hell was the worst, but not only consequence of sin. If there were a sufficient response to her pleas, she said, "many souls will be saved, and there will be peace." If not, though the war then raging would end, "another and worse one will begin in the reign of Pius XI."(103)

The Mother of God, like her dear sons Pope Benedict XV and Emperor Charles, had to plead and beg for peace. Jesus Christ and His mother coerce no one. But in the end she—the fragile. exquisite Lily of Israel, "Mary whom God kissed in Galilee"(104) —while pleading, conquers. In this hour, as always in her life on earth and even in Heaven until the end of the world shall come, Mary of Nazareth spoke both as victim and as victor. Her soft, sweetly firm words dropped like rocks into the stream of time, diverting forever the course of history:

> I come to ask the consecration of Russia to my Immaculate Heart and the Communion of reparation on the first Saturdays. If they listen to my requests, Russia will be converted and there will be peace. If not, she will scatter her errors through the world, provoking wars and persecutions of the Church. The good will be martyrized, the Holy Father will have much to suffer, various nations will be annihilated. In the end my Immaculate Heart will triumph. The Holy Father will consecrate Russia to me, and it will be converted, and a certain period of peace will be granted to the world.(105)

This for Russia—of which Lucia, Jacinta and Francisco knew absolutely nothing, where the triumph of Lenin's mighty evil was still five months distant—and for the world. Then, for their own sunny, troubled little land, hardly noticed, hardly remembered in the midst of the colossal struggle of the world war, a glorious promise, the like of which has never been given to any other nation or people on earth: "In Portugal the dogma of the Faith will always be kept."(106)

Then again the Rosary:

> When you say the Rosary, say after each mystery, "O my Jesus, pardon us and deliver us from the fire of hell. Draw all souls to heaven, expecially those in most need."(107)

Finally a last secret, which has never been revealed. Lucia has not told it even to her confessors. Later she communicated it to the Pope, with Our Lady's instructions that it not be opened for many years. It is believed to have been read by Pope John XXIII. He did not reveal it.

The Cova da Iria and all within it had fallen absolutely silent. Lucia, pale as a ghost, watched the Lady depart as usual, toward the east.

* * * * * *

July 13, 1917 was a Friday. That Sunday, the 15th, the British guns began to boom from the Flanders trenches, their shells making great gouts in the soft black earth, which gradually filled with water. In Petrograd that Sunday the First Machine-Gun Regiment, which had an unusually large percentage of its rank and file influenced by the Communists, turned out to hear Trotsky. Some of the units of the regiment had just been ordered to the front. Reception of the orders coincided witht he first unvarnished reports in Petrograd newspapers of the complete failure of the highly touted "Kerensky offensive," undertaken on both the northern and southern parts of the eastern front during the first two weeks of July.

Trotsky was a magnificent speaker. Time and again during

the coming months he was to demonstrate his power to sway crowds of workingmen or soldiers. Lenin held and dominated crowds by the sheer force of his personality, by the shattering imperatives of his irresistible will. Trotsky was more genuinely persuasive; he was a master of every kind of appeal to an audience, from real argument to emotional exhortation. His message to the First Machine-Gun Regiment July 15 was simply the consistent Communist line ever since Lenin's arrival at the Finland station in Petrograd in April: All power to the Soviets! But it struck an even more responsive chord now that the Provisional Government had so conspicuously, almost ludicrously failed in war, and was about to risk these men's lives in an evidently losing cause.

The next day the machine gunners demanded action, not talk. They marched on the Communist Party headquarters at the Kshesinskaya Palace to launch an immediate major armed demonstration on the streets of Petrograd in support of full power to the Soviets. This was more than Lenin and Trotsky had bargained for. They did not yet have enough solid support throughout the country to risk a full-scale confrontation in the seizure of supreme power. Lenin was not even in Petrograd, but in Finland recuperating from a slight illness. Trotsky had not intended his speech to the First Machine-Gun Regiment as a signal for an immediate uprising. But when he and others tried to restrain the mobs that evening, they proved for the moment uncontrollable.

On Tuesday, July 17, twenty thousand armed sailors from Kronstadt arrived to support the demonstration. Lenin arrived also, urging restraint while promising ultimate victory. Confused masses poured into the streets and surrounded the Tauride Palace; there was much random shooting and several hundred casualties. A mob seized the Socialist Revolutionary minister of agriculture, Victor Chernov; a worker shook his fist in Chernov's face, shouting: "Take power, you son of a bitch, when they give it to you."(108) Trotsky had to rescue him.

Without leadership the uprising, which Lenin accurately termed "something considerably more than a demonstration and

less than a revolution,''(109) burned itself out by the evening of
July 17. The Soviet had not endorsed the armed demonstration in
its favor; the Provisional Government viewed the unsuccessful
outbreak as its great opportunity to discredit the Communists and
eliminate them as a significant factor in Russian politics.
Documents were released to show that Lenin was a German agent.
The testimony came from unreliable sources; what truth there was
in it was drawn from the indubitable fact that the Germans had
helped Lenin get back into Russia, by the sealed train and with
money. But it found fertile ground for acceptance among many
Russians, including workers and soldiers, who were by and large
still passionately anti-German despite the growing sentiment for
peace, and were disgusted for various reasons by the failure of the
''July days'' uprising. Kerensky issued orders for the arrest of
Lenin, Zinoviev, and Kamenev.

Disguised as a workman named Konstantin Ivanov, moving
from apartment to apartment in the workingmen's Vyborg quarter
of Petrograd, spending no more than a few hours in each hiding
place, Lenin considered for several days giving himself up. He was
confident he could win his case in an open trial, by the force of his
will and reputation and the evident totality of his revolutionary
commitment; but he was not at all sure that, once helpless in
prison, he would live to be tried. An effort was made to obtain from
the government some kind of guarantee of Lenin's personal safety
if he went to prison. When this was not forthcoming in any
satisfactory form, all thought of surrendering was abandoned.

With Stalin's help, Lenin and Zinoviev escaped from
Petrograd, jumping on a freight train at two o'clock in the morning
just as it was leaving the Finland station. They were unobserved.
They got off the train in the darkness at the little station of Razliv
near the Finnish border, still unobserved, and made their way to
the house of a revolutionary named Emelianov, who had known
Lenin since 1905. For three weeks Emelianov hid Lenin and
Zinoviev in a hollowed-out hayrick in the forest, warm and bright
now at the height of the northern summer, where Lenin read the
Petrograd newspapers every day and commented on events
reported there in articles which he sent in to Petrograd for

publication in a day or two. Very few in Russia knew where he was;
the government never found him.

******

On July 24 Pacelli presented a formal Papal mediation offer to
the German government, based on Bethmann-Hollweg's preliminary response of June: full restoration of Belgian independence
and territorial integrity under international guarantees, with
Germany's colonies to be restored in return; international arms
limitation, freedom of the seas, and an international court of
arbitration to be approved in principle; and a peace conference to
settle the very difficult border questions, notably those involving
Alsace-Lorraine and the South Tyrol. The Kaiser was definitely in
favor of pursuing the Papal peace initiative; but Michaelis was not
Bethmann-Hollweg. Michaelis wanted peace negotiations—as
did, even more emphatically, the Reichstag, which had passed a
peace resolution July 19—but Ludendorff at army headquarters
had what amounted to an absolute veto on any such proceedings. It
soon became clear, if Michaelis had ever really doubted it, that
Ludendorff would use that veto to prevent any significant
concessions, including the full restoration of Belgium.

But for the time being the parties temporized; and because of
the initial very favorable response from Bethmann-Hollweg, even
though he was now gone, Pacelli thought for a brief period that the
Germans might be truly ready for peace.

******

On the last day of July the next holocaust on the Western front
began. Two hundred thousand Englishmen stood ready in the
Flemish trenches, their backs on shattered Ypres, facing
Passchendaele ridge and the Gheluvelt plateau (as a sixty-foot
elevation just on the German side of the line, mountainous in
dead-flat Flanders, was grandly called). In General Jacob's Second
Corps the point division for the attack was the 30th, Manchester
and Liverpool boys, survivors of those who had been through the
horrible slaughter on the Somme. Here was more of the

same—except that this terrain was even flatter and even muddier.

A few primitive tanks accompanied the assault. Barely able to crawl at the speed of one mile per hour, soon stuck in the mud or knocked out by anti-tank guns, they accomplished nothing whatever. During the morning the creeping artillery barrage steadily advanced, while the infantry it was supposed to cover found themselves pinned down. As usual, there was no effective coordination or communication between the two military arms. By ten o'clock in the morning the artillery fire was so far foward of the line of actual advance as to be useless. Advances were no more than 500 yards, if that. The "inaccurate" German artillery raked the attackers mercilessly; strong point after strong point in the defenses proved impregnable; whole units were lost in nightmarish tangles of fallen trees, barbed wire, shell holes and bursting shrapnel. Only carrier pigeons could get through, and the little birds beating through the shrieking air brought message after message of ruin and disaster.

By afternoon some advances of up to a mile had occurred; but since they were isolated, their only effect was to create salients in the line which could then be enfiladed by fire from both flanks as well as from in front. Some of the salients consequently had to be abandoned that very day. In some assault units casualties reached seventy per cent.

At one o'clock in the afternoon, under a cold west wind and scudding gray clouds, it began to rain. By four o'clock the rain was torrential. There was no place in that land, its natural state a swamp, its drainage ditches ruined by three years of war, its water table already high, for the water flow away. The underlying stratum of clay was almost impervious. So the water flowed into the trenches—and stayed there. Its level steadily rose.

Night fell. No moonlight gleamed; no star flickered. The rain poured down. The sky was utterly black, pitch-black, coal-black, a vast inky curtain. Periodically during the night the Germans fired into the trenches and pillboxes which had been carried by the assailants, having pinpionted their locations precisely during the years they had held them. All through the night fierce hand-to-hand battles kept breaking out as the Germans came back to the trenches and pillboxes which had been theirs, trying to regain them.

By the next morning, the first of August, by Haig's own admission some of his men had begun to die by drowning in the mud—and not only the wounded. The attack was suspended for two days, in hope that the rain would let up. But then it would be resumed—regardless.

August 1917

Arturo da Oliveira Santos was Administrator of the Council of Ourem, the town seven miles from Fatima which was the administrative center of the district including Fatima and its surrounding countryside. He was a young man of 33 who had risen rapidly in the anti-clerical government which had taken power in Portugal in 1910, overthrowing the ancient Catholic monarchy, exiling the Cardinal Patriarch of Lisbon, torturing the future Bishop of Leiria so that he was crippled for life, and seizing much of the property of the Catholic Church throughout the country. Santos had established in Ourem a lodge of the Grand Orient Masons, a group he had joined in the year of the revolution, 1910; in 1911 its chief for Portugal had predicted that within a few years there would be no more young Portuguese interested in becoming Catholic priests. Three of Santos' children were named Democracy, Republic, and Liberty. He was a blacksmith; he called his smithy the Forge of Progress. He hated the Catholic Church and despised the very thought of the supernatural and miraculous.

Shortly before the expected return of the Blessed Virgin Mary to the Cova da Iria on August 13, Santos sent formal notices to Manuel Pedro Marto and Antonio Abobora, Lucia's father, to bring their children who had been disturbing the public peace to him in Ourem for questioning.

Marto refused to send his children such a distance, since they were unused to riding and could not walk so far; instead, he came himself. Abobora, who had never believed his daughter's story, came grumbling with Lucia riding a burro, from which she fell three times on the way.

Santos questioned Lucia about the secret told to her at the July apparition, ending with a threat in the presence of both men to kill her if she did not tell it. Then he let her go.

By August 12, a Sunday, pilgrims had already begun to gather at the Cova da Iria and around the cottages where the three children lived. Santos himself came to the Marto home to demand that the children not go to the Cova da Iria the next day. They said they must go; the Queen of Heaven had commanded them. Santos suggested they discuss the matter againt the next morning with the Fatima parish priest, Father Ferreira—whom he thought he could pressure.

He could, and apparently he did; because on the morning of August 13, when the children were brought to Father Ferreira, he accused them of lying and threatened them with Hell for it. But the Blessed Virgin Mary herself had promised them Heaven; they were not to be moved.

Physical force alone remained. Santos put the three children into his wagon, cracked the whip over his horse, and clattered off toward Ourem with blankets thrown over the children to hide them from any of the pilgrims who might recognize them on the road. By noon, the hour of Our Lady's appearing, they were in his custody at Ourem.

By then six thousand people were assembled in the Cova da Iria. A faint murmur, like very distant thunder, was heard; then something came like a white shadow, glimmering, gossamer, floating down upon the little tree where all the apparitions had occurred. But this time no one was there to recognize or greet the Lady; a moment later the wraith-like cloud rose again from the tree and faded into the sky. As the bemused people looked about, they found themselves and all the surrounding earth and foliage bathed in brilliant rainbow colors.

Had Arturo da Oliveira Santos defeated the Mother of God?

He had not defeated the three children. When they remained steadfast in their account of the Lady, he threw them into the town jail, in a filthy common room with local criminals. There, kneeling on the floor together, they prayed the Rosary. Many of the prisoners joined them. Afterwards, when Jacinta cried for her mother, the prisoners sang and danced for her, to end her tears and make her smile. Natural and supernatural good touched the Ourem prison that day; at least one thief was permanently converted by the experience. Later in the day Santos took the children out of the jail, again demanded their secret, and when he was again refused, announced that he would boil them in oil. The children were separated; each one was told that the others had died in agony. It seems they believed it.

They were ten, nine, and seven years old.

They held firm.

On August 15, the feast of the Assumption of Our Lady, Santos had to admit defeat and send the children home.

Their parents had been in anguish, for no one had been able to tell them where their children were. The parishioners of Fatima, who knew that Santos had taken them away and suspected Father Ferreira of complicity since they had originally been taken from his rectory, were very angry both with their pastor and with Santos. Their anger increased when the children were dropped without apology or explanation at the rectory by one of Santos' men, immediately after the holy day Mass. After greeting his children with tears in his eyes, Manuel Pedro Marto found first Father Ferreira and then even Santos appealing for his help in quelling the crowd. He stepped before them to speak:

> Behave yourselves! Some of you are shouting against the Prior, some against the Administrator, some against the Regidor. Nobody is to blame here. The fault is one of unbelief, and all has been permitted by the power of the One above!(110)

The world was at war; but Manuel Pedro Marto—and the Blessed Virgin Mary—wanted no war in Fatima.

On Sunday, August 19, Lucia and Francisco and Francisco's brother John were pasturing their sheep on the northern slope of The Head, very near where Lucia and Jacinta and Francisco had seen the Angel of Peace the summer before. Suddenly Lucia felt that Our Lady was coming. She sent John to fetch Jacinta. The came a flash of light, and then—as soon as Jacinta arrived—the wonderful white radiance. The Lady stood, this time, on a small bush.

She told them she wished them to come again to the Cova da Iria on the thirteenth of September, and to continue saying the Rosary daily. She repeated her promise of a great miracle on October 13. Lucia asked her what she should do with the money which many of the pilgrims had left at the Cova da Iria August 13 with Maria Carreira. Mary said it should be used to begin the building of a chapel there. (In her apparition in Mexico in 1531, as Our Lady of Guadalupe, Mary had asked that a church be built on the hill of Tepeyac, where she had appeared; at one of her apparitions to St. Bernadette at Lourdes in 1858, she asked that the faithful come there in procession.) She concluded by asking again for prayers and sacrifices in reparation for sin. Then she disappeared into the east.

The children brought home the branches from the little bush on The Head upon which the Blessed Virgin Mary had stood. Manuel Pedro Marto always remembered the penetrating sweetness that emanated from those branches; he called it "magnificent." Even Lucia's doubting mother admitted there was something very special about this fragrance.

Several days later the three children found a rough, heavy piece of rope in the lone street of the hamlet of Aljustrel near their homes. They cut pieces from it to wear as girdles around their waists, next to the skin, so that they might offer the pain and discomfort from these improvised hair shirts, for the conversion of sinners.

******

On August 12, the day before the Blessed Virgin Mary was to return to the Cova da Iria, Pope Benedict XV dispatched a note to the government of each of the belligerent powers in the world war, over his own signature. The note asked:

> Shall, then, the civilized world be nought but a field of death? And shall Europe, so glorious and flourishing, rush as though driven by universal madness towards the abyss, and lend her hand to her own suicide?(111)

Then it called for peace on the basis of seven principles: (1) substitution of "the moral force of right" for "the material force of arms"; (2) limitation of armaments; (3) compulsory arbitration of international disputes; (4) full freedom of the seas; (5) renunciation of all claims to war indemnities; (6) evacuation and restoration of all territories conquered during the war; (7) review of the border territorial disputes, such as those involving Alsace-Lorraine and the South Tyrol, "in a conciliatory spirit."

This eminently sound and fair proposal was handled very much as Arturo da Oliveira Santos had handled the Fatima children: questioned, locked up, threatened, and finally dismissed with contempt. Only Emperor Charles—and King Ferdinand of Bulgaria, hardly a major factor in the war—welcomed it unreservedly.

The first response came from British Foreign Minister Arthur Balfour on August 21, declaring that nothing could be done until the Central Powers "admitted their guilt in regard to Belgium" and not only restored Belgian independence but pledged large economic reparations. (The Pope too had made it very clear that he insisted on the full restoration of Belgium's independence—but not on reparations.) Even this very tentative and well-hedged response was too much for Great Britain's chief European allies, France and Italy; both Ribot and Sonnino vehemently objected to any written communication whatever with the Pope on questions of war and peace. In Germany, many Reichstag deputies strongly urged an unconditional German guarantee of the restoration of Belgium, but they could obtain no commitment of this kind from the government in the looming shadow of the irrecocilable Ludendorff.

It was left to U.S. President Woodrow Wilson, the idealist, the peace-lover so reluctantly forced into the war, to deliver the decisive, smashing blow to the Papal peace offer. His first response to it was to say of Benedict: "What does he want to butt in for?"(112) Then in a full written reply August 27, Wilson simply refused to deal with the German government in its existing form under any circumstances—a refusal he was later to apply to Charles of Austria as well.

The object of this war is to deliver the free peoples of the world from the menace and the actual power of a vast military establishment controlled by an irresponsible government which, having secretly planned to dominate the world, proceeded to carry the plan out . . . This power is not the German people. It is the ruthless master of the German people. It is no business of ours how that great people came under its control or submitted with temporary zest to the domination of its purpose, but it is our business to see to it that the history of the rest of the world is no longer left to its handling.

To deal with such a power by way of peace upon the plan proposed by His Holiness the Pope would, so far as we can see, involve a recuperation of its strength and a renewal of its policy, would make it necessary to create a permanent hostile combination of nations against the German people who are its instruments . . .

The test, therefore, of every plan of peace is this: Is it based upon the faith of all the peoples involved or merely upon the word of an ambitious and intriguing government on the one hand and of a group of free peoples on the other? . . .

We cannot take the word of the present rulers of Germany as a guaranty of anything that is to endure.(113)

Yet is had been Woodrow Wilson himself who had said, less than five months before, that entry into the war by the United States would mean "that we should lose our heads along with the rest, and stop weighing right and wrong. . .an attempt to reconstruct a peacetime civilization with war standards."

Woodrow Wilson had had the intellectual stature to see the likelihood of that result, once the United States was in the war. He did not have the moral stature to refrain from participating, or even taking the lead, in bringing that result to pass.

******

In Flanders there was a British tank officer named Baker-Carr. One day in August Baker-Carr was called to British general headquarters, well to the rear, to explain this new form of warfare. His lecture on its priniciples was very well received. Then, at lunch, he told the headquarters officers what was really happening at the front. The Passchendaele offensive, he said, was "dead as mutton."

A shocked silence fell. Officers at General Haig's headquarters simply did not talk that way. Brigadier-General John Davidson, Haig's director of operations, called Baker-Carr into his office.

> "I am very upset by what you said at lunch, Baker. If it had been some junior officer, it wouldn't have mattered so much, but a man of your knowledge and experience had no right to speak as you did."
>
> "You asked me how things really were and I told you frankly."
>
> "But what you say is impossible."
>
> "It isn't. Nobody has any idea of the conditions up there."
>
> "But they can't be as bad as you make out."
>
> "Have you been there yourself?"
>
> "No."
>
> "Has anyone in O.A. been there?"
>
> "No."
>
> "Well, then, if you don't believe me, it would be as well to send someone up there to find out."(114)

No one was sent. The killing went on. When August ended, the British had suffered 75,000 casualties in Flanders and the Germans 50,000. No significant gains whatever had been made. But no one would call off the offensive.

September 1917

September was the sixth month since the Petrograd revolution that overthrew the Czar. During all those six months the slow, inexorable tide of social disintegration had been flowing through the vastness of the Russian empire. Like a towering sand dune undermined by water which had never before reached to its base, the whole public and social order of Russia softened, crumbled and gradually slid into the deep.

This was not primarily the work of the Communists, nor of any political combination or faction; but only the Communists welcomed the disintegration unreservedly, aided the undermining trends and movement wherever they could, and rejoiced over every slippage and collapse. From his dramatic April arrival at Petrograd's Finland station through the build-up of his party's organization in May and June to the abortive uprising in July and his concealment during August in Emelianov's hay-rick and later in various hiding places in Finland, Lenin kept his finger on the pulse of Russia, his razor-keen intellect charting her course toward the ultimate breakdown that alone could bring him and his party and his cause to power. From April to August the national membership of the Communist Party had grown from 80,000 to 200,000 and its membership in Petrograd from 16,000 to 36,000. In the midst of the turmoil, danger and apparent disaster of the July riots, Lenin had cast a coldly unmoved eye upon the future, and declared that the Communist revolution in Russia would come that autumn.

The central truth was that there was nothing to hold the huge country together. The Czar had been the linch-pin. With the Czar removed, without a successor, no government had any basis in law or tradition. Some version of the Lockean theory of the "state of nature" and government by consent of the governed could perhaps be applied—though rather unrealistically—to the Constituent Assembly, an all-Russian representative body to be created by the national elections to establish a permanent new government. But the elections for the Constituent Assembly had not yet been held; their date had been repeatedly postponed. Meanwhile the curious dual system of Provisional Government and Soviets continued, the one a mixture of survivors from the old and now virtually forgotten Imperial Duma and new appointees, the other increasingly a product of mob action among workers and soldiers. Neither had any legal basis or commanded anything approaching a consensus of national respect.

Alexander Kerensky, head of the Provisional Government, had emerged from relative obscurity in the Czar's Duma on that wild March day at the Tauride Palace facing fifty thousand men who had made a revolution but didn't know what to do with it, taking charge simply and solely by the power of his oratory. With the possible exception of Trotsky, Kerensky was the best orator in Russia in 1917. But an orator was all he was. He could only ride the mighty wave of revolution like a surfer; it was totally beyond his control. Yet such was the intoxication of those frantic months that through all the long years of life in exile that were to be his—he was eighty-nine years old when he died in New York in 1970—Alexander Kerensky would not, perhaps could not, ever bring himself to admit that he had never really governed Russia. From March until November 1917, no one really governed Russia.

It was not full anarchy, a conditon that among civilized men exists only in books on political science, because real living men will not tolerate it. But it was as close to anarchy as the modern world has ever seen, or is ever likely to see, in a great nation. Even the French Revolution here offers no real parallel. From the beginning, revolutionary France had an elected national assembly which governed in the name of the people. Russia in 1917 had nothing of the sort. And revolutionary France produced the finest army the world had seen for two hundred years, while in revolutionary Russia the army disintegrated.

The reason, of course, was the First World War. The daily horror, the "living hell" of the trenches, that the young men of every other belligerent nation numbly endured because the whole weight and shape and habit and custom of the public order demanded it and secured it, making even the French army mutinies of 1917 only a brief interlude in the pattern of obedience, exacted its ultimate price in Russia when the Russian public order broke down. The soldiers would no longer fight. In ever-growing numbers during the spring and summer of 1917, despite the confusion and near-chaos of public transportation, they simply went home. By late August there had been, since the March revolution, *two million desertions* out of an army of seven million. Desertions continued by the thousands daily; there was no way to stop them. Officers who antagonized their mutinous men, such as by attempting too vigorously to re-establish order and discipline, were shot out of hand, with virtually no fear of punishment. The troops who remained on line did so solely to prevent Russia from being overrun by the Germans; a strong anti-German sentiment still existed. But they intended to do that in their own way. The officers could only function at all by going through a bewildering maze of soldiers' committees elected by different units, which varied in their character and policy as much as their members individually differed from the members of other committees of their kind. Much depended on whether there was a Communist on the committee—as there often was. No real authority remained in the army of Russia.

An equally fearsome breakdown had occurred upon the land.

Upon the enormous expanses of the farmland of Russia, Stolypin's reforms had come too late. No more than ten per cent of the peasants had enough land of their own to support themselves and their families above the level of dire poverty. The great bulk of the land was divided between the estates of the large land-owners and the tracts in communal ownership by the villages. The peasants had yearned for land of their own, dreamed of land of their own, for generations. They had been restrained in their land hunger by fear of the government's troops and by love for, and loyalty to the Czar. Now there were no government troops and there was no Czar. The peasants struck, fired by all the accumulated grievances of the centuries since Genghis Khan and his Mongols, "the devil's horsemen", had made themselves the ruthless overlords of Russia and distorted the whole development of the Russian state towards tyranny, seven hundred years before.

The full story of the ensuing horror has never been, and probably never will be told. It is composed of ten thousand local tragedies of burning and looting and smashing and killing, of old scores settled and envy slaked, of just and imaginary grievances all jumbled together and avenged in blood and ashes, each one a bit in a mosaic which it has never served anyone's interest to assemble, and for which most of the needed records either never existed, or vanished in the cataclysm. One bit of the mosaic—a tale told by Harrison Salisbury in his history of the Russian Revolution, from interviews and unpublished manuscripts—will suffice to give an impression of the whole. In Tambov province was found the model farm of Lotarevo, an internationally famous center of agricultural and livestock development, owned by the Vyazemsky family. In 1917 Lotarevo was managed by Boris Vyazemsky, a brilliant and popular young man of 33, well-liked by the neighbors of Lotarevo as well as in Petrograd and Moscow, a liberal in politics, a member of the Consitutional Democratic party. He worked closely and harmoniously with the regional committee and its peasant representatives which was set up in the wake of the March revolution, in that area as in many others, to fill the vacuum left by the collapse of the imperial government and to prevent anarchy. But as the summer of 1917 wore on, the mood of the people began to change. Old grievances against members of the Vyazemsky family were remembered, though none involved Boris. A Communist agitator appeared in the area, urging an attack on Lotarevo. One August morning a peasant mob came to Lotarevo. Boris refused to flee. He talked with the farmers. But they wanted him out; they wanted his land. The Communist encouraged them. A farmer said to Boris: "Have it as you will, Your Excellency, but we are for Lenin and we will not retreat from him a single step."(115) They decided to order Boris Vyazemsky shipped to the front to fight as a common soldier.

The next day a train full of deserters from the front pulled into the railroad station near Lotarevo where Boris was being held. The deserters battered down the door of the room where he was confined and tore him to pieces.

At Lotarevo the specially bred livestock were killed and their barns demolished. The great house was pillaged from ceiling to cellar, until only a bare shell stood.

When a national Congress of Soviets of Peasants' Deputies met in Petrograd in early June, it adopted a model resolution for the expropriation of land based on 242 resolutions which local peasant committees had used for this purpose and brought for presentation to the congress. It began:

> The right of private property in land is abolished forever; land can be neither sold nor bought nor leased nor pledged nor alienated in any way. All land . . . is taken over without compensation as the property of the whole people and passes over to the use of those who work on it.(116)

In November, Lenin was to take over this part of the model land expropriation resolution of the Congress of Peasants' Soviets, word for word, and use it as the foundation for the Communist administration of all land in Russia—the greatest land seizure in history, which has been responsible for untold human misery for more than sixty years.

Such was the spectacle of Russia in early September 1917 when General Lavr Georgevich Kornilov, commander-in-chief of what was left of the Russian army, and several of his principal officers made a last desperate bid to halt the collapse and save their country.

Kornilov had been born in Siberia, the son of a Cossack officer, who eventually had to leave the army because of the very low pay he received due to his humble origins, and go to work as a government clerk. As a very young officer Lavr Georgevich had been posted to distant Turkestan; he had married a totally undistinguished Cossack girl. There was nothing whatever of the aristocrat in Kornilov. The army was his life. He had risen purely

by merit, courage, and determination. He was passionately
patriotic. Now he saw his army and his country dissolving before
his eyes.

Kerensky had appoint Kornilov commander-in-chief August 1
after the total failure of General Brusilov's offensive in early July.
He demanded, as an indispensable condition of his acceptance of
the command, the restoration of military discipline and specifically
of the power of officers to punish disobedient, mutinous and
criminal soldiers by summary courts-martial and, where necessary, by the death penalty, Kerensky promised him this, but could
not deliver it. Kornilov was told that the Communists were
planning an uprising in Petrograd on September 12, six months
after the revolution that overthrew the Czar. (Actually there is no
evidence that anyone planned such an uprising then.) He moved to
forestall the reported coup by placing a cavalry corps consisting of
two Cossack divisions and the "Savage Division" of Muslim hill
tribesmen from the Caucasus in position for a quick move on
Petrograd. Once this corps took over Petrograd, he told his
associate and supporter General Lukomsky, he would hang Lenin
and "disperse the Soviet of Workers' and Soldiers' Deputies so
that it would never reassemble."(117) Rodzyanko, the former
president of the Duma who had been the last to try to stave off the
March revolution by urging at least minimal reforms on the Czar,
telegraphed Kornilov: "In this threatening hour of heavy trial, all
thinking Russia looks to you with hope and faith."(118) Late in
August Kornilov came to the meeting of the Moscow State
Conference, a vast body of more than 2400 delegates; before
speaking to them, he went to pray in the Chapel of the Iberian
Virgin, the most famous shrine in Moscow, where the Czars had
always gone to pray before their coronations.

It is all too characteristic of modern historiography that
virtually every account of the Russian Revolution and of Kornilov's
attempted coup states or implies that Kornilov went to the shrine
of the Iberian Virgin because he sought to link himself in some
ritualistic quasi-political way with the Czars who had prayed there
before being crowned—despite the fact that Kornilov is certainly
known to have been totally opposed (as virtually everyone in

Russia was) to any restoration of the Romanov dynasty. It seems to have occurred to no one even to consider the possibility that he was actually there to beg the Blessed Virgin Mary's help.

She had said:

> If they listen to my requests, Russia will be converted and there will be peace. If not, she will scatter her errors through the world, provoking wars and persecutions of the Church.

On this small dark man with narrow half-Oriental eyes and a black mustache, superlatively brave but totally lacking in political experience, praying to the Blessed Virgin Mary in her most revered chapel in Moscow, the burden of the war and the world and the future now descended. Surely he must have felt the crushing weight of it. His prayers rose to the Lady who had come back to the Fatima children in Portugal just eight days before.

But not all prayers are answered—at least, not as we men in our very limited vision can see and surmise. And, so far as this world can tell, General Kornilov's were not.

Through a series of tragi-comical blunders and misunderstandings, Kerensky learned of Kornilov's plans on September 8. The next day he ordered his dismissal from command. Kornilov and his principal subordinates refused to accept the dismissal, and Kornilov ordered the three previously prepared cavalry divisions to march on Petrograd.

Why he did not take command of them in person has never been explained. It was certainly not for lack of courage; Lavr Georgevich Kornilov had the heart of a lion, and he was later to die in battle against the Communists. It seems to have been primarily a lack of anticipation of the inevitable difficulties and an unjustified expectation of widespread support in Petrograd. Supreme army headquarters at Mogilev remained much the best place from which to direct the operations of the whole army; and the possibility that his divisions, on their way to Petrograd without him, might be halted or subverted enroute, and his communication with them cut off, never seems to have occurred to Kornilov, who obviously had grave deficiencies as a strategist.

But that he knew fully what was at stake, is evident from his extraordinary proclamation of September 10, which included this poignant paragraph:

> The solemn certainty of the doom of this our country compels me in these terrible times to call upon all her loyal sons to save their dying native land. All within whom a Russian heart still beats, all who believe in God, go into the churches and pray to Our Lord for the greatest possible miracle, the salvation of our dear country.(119)

The dying words and the deathless hope ring down the years. Kornilov's own prayers, unanswered, were soon stilled in this world by his death; but the prayers he asked for are offered to this day, in Russia and by all who hear and heed Our Lady of Fatima.

In Petrograd all parties joined in vehement opposition to Kornilov. Even the Constitutional Democrats, among whom he had many supporters, did not now dare to speak in his favor. Lenin from his hiding place directed the Communist strategy: "We will fight Kornilov, but we will not support Kerensky."(120) A Committee for Struggle with Counterrevolution was set up with members from all the revolutionary parties and from the Petrograd Soviet, the labor unions, and the peasants; the Committee in turn approved a workers' militia and, primarily through the Communists, equipped 25,000 of them with rifles in a few days, and many with machine guns. The three divisions Kornilov had sent to take Petrograd were travelling by rail; seventy miles south of the capital their trains came to a halt as they found long stretches of track thoroughly torn up by the railroad workers—too long and too thoroughly for quick repair. The wires to Mogilev were cut. The corps commander, General Krymov, was indecisive if not incompetent, and now he had no way to get in touch with Kornilov; he was on his own. His divisions encamped.

The Petrograd Soviet promptly sent carefully chosen delegates to subvert the Cossacks and the "Savage Division"—delegates who were themselves mostly Cossacks and Caucasian Muslims. Under all normal circumstances, and many abnormal ones, such troops—genuine volunteers and professionals—could have been counted on to repel agitators like these with scorn. But under the conditions of the First World War and of leaderless Russia in

Rasputin's wake, morale was like an eggshell, cracking at a touch. The troops listened to the men from the Soviet. After a day's debate, on September 12 they decided not to march further toward Petrograd; and on September 13 they submitted unconditionally to the Provisional Government and sent a delegation of their own humbly begging the pardon of the Petrograd Soviet for having been misled. General Krymov shot himself. Kerensky took personal command of the army, appointed the former commander-in-chief General Alexeyev as his chief of staff, and sent him to Mogilev to arrest Kornilov and several of the other generals involved with him in the abortive coup. The arrests were made on September 14.

* * * * * *

On September 13 the German Chancellor Michaelis placed before the Kaiser a draft reply to the Papal peace note, full of honeyed platitudes, but nowhere mentioning Belgium, since at a crown council meeting two days earlier the Kaiser, under heavy pressure from his generals and admirals, had said he could not immediately give up all of Belgium. The Kaiser signed the reply. Foreign Minister von Kuhlmann was told there was a specific decision *not* to give the Pope any German statement on Belgium. Benedict XV had always insisted that a German pledge to restore fully the territory of Belgium, which she had so unjustly invaded, was an absolutely essential prerequisite for peace. The Papal peace initiative was dead.

Also on September 13, the Communists finally gained for the first time a substantial majority in the Petrograd Soviet; and the British in Flanders, under Haig, began the preliminary bombardment for yet another massive assault on the impregnable German front near Passchendaele.

That was the day of Blessed Virgin Mary's fifth return to the Cova da Iria. The largest crowd yet to assemble there awaited her coming with Lucia, Jacinta and Francisco. In the crowd were a number of priests, including two friends, Father Joao Quaresma and Father Manuel da Silva. Here is Father Quaresma's report:

To my great astonishment I saw clearly and distinctly a luminous
globe that moved from the east toward the west, slowly and
majestically gliding down across the distance . . .
"What do you think of that globe?" I asked of my friend . . .
"That it was Our Lady," he replied without hesitation. It was
my conviction also. The little shepherds looked on the Mother of
God herself; to us was granted the grace to see the carriage
which had transported her.(121)

Afterwards, Father Quaresma found many others who had
seen the luminous globe.

This time the Lady spoke very briefly:

Continue to say the Rosary to bring about the end of the war.
In October Our Lord will come also, and Our Lady of the Sorrows
of Carmel, and Saint Joseph with the Child Jesus, to bless the
world. God is content with your sacrifices, but does not wish you
to sleep with the rope—wear it only during the day.(122)

Once again she promised a great miracle in October.

Writing from Helsinki in Finland, as September drew to a
close, Lenin was calling for immediate Communist action to seize
power—today Russia, tomorrow the world.

The Bolsheviki can and must take the state power into their
hands. . . . An insurrection must rest on a turning point in the
history of a growing revolution, when the activity of the leading
ranks of the people is greatest and when the waverings in the
ranks of the enemies and of the weak, half-hearted, undecided
friends of the revolution are greatest.(123)

In Russia there are still great resources both material and
spiritual for a truly revolutionary war; there are 99 chances out of
100 that the Germans will at least give us a truce. And to secure
a truce at present—this means already to conquer *the whole
world.*(124)

Across a continent, across a cosmos, across the immense
wreckage of Western Christian civilization, they faced each
other, the ultimate surviving antagonists of the apocalyptic year
1917: the girl-woman all in radiant white, with the lovely voice and
the gentle, serious mien, Queen of Heaven and earth, Mother of
God, who had promised that Her Immaculate Heart would one day
prevail in Russia and bring peace to all the world; and Vladimir

Ilyich Ulyanov called Lenin, with his jarring voice and his whipcrack laugh and his bald bullet head and his mighty brain, ready to take Russia and the whole world for himself and his atheist, materialist creed, certain that the time had come for him to strike and to win.

Yet he too was her son, though he had put her out of his life since the days he had cherished the traditional Russian Christmas as a child, and the currents of her love and, above all, the love of her Son Who is God, thrust ceaselessly against the iron bars of his heart.

October 1917

On September 20, on September 26, on October 4, like the relentless clanking steps of a robot, General Sir Douglas Haig hurled his British troops through the oceanic mire of drowning Flanders against the long-prepared German lines. Wild claims of victory re-echoed after each attack in official statements and in the subservient or bemused press; at one mad moment during the October 4 attack Charteris, Haig's intelligence chief, cried joyously to General Harington standing beside him: "Now we have them on the run! Get up the cavalry!"(125) But in sober fact, the average advance in this attack was 700 yards, at the cost of 26,000 British casualties—one per inch gained. Not much had changed since the Battle of the Somme. Most certainly, nobody was "on the run."

From October 4 to October 7 it rained, a constant succession of heavy showers. Men could move only on duckboards. In every shell-hole and trench the water rose. Vehicles and cannon could not move at all; animals sent to pull them often drowned in the mud. On October 7 the showers turned into a torrential, unrelenting downpour. That evening Haig called a council of war.

His two principal subordinates, Generals Plumer and Gough, who had supported the Passchendaele offensive up to this point, both told him flatly that the campaign should be ended immediately. Even the mad Charteris had confided to his diary that day (as the rain poured down): "Unless we get fine weather for all this month, there is no chance of clearing the coast."(126) (The next day he was back to his usual self, predicting seizure of the Belgian coast and victory in the war—by Christmas.) But Haig was fixated on Passchendaele ridge. He had been hammering toward it for more than two months, but it still remained untaken. However, it was now little more than a mile in front of his most advanced outposts. He was determined to encamp there for the winter. It did not matter what anyone else thought about it. As for the weather, he hoped it would improve. As for the terrain, it was "not yet impossible."(127) As for the French, they could not be depended upon, but he could win the war without them. As for the Russians, they would stay in the war. As for the Germans, they would be able to put only 179 divisions on line at the Western front in 1918 (the actual number proved to be 210, an underestimate of half a million men) and very soon they would "gladly accept such terms of peace as the Allies might offer."(128) As for the Americans, "there must be no thought of staying our hand until America puts an army in the field next year."(129) The attacks would continue.

The morning of October 8 was sunny; another full-scale British assault was set for the following dawn. But as afternoon wore on, the dreaded gray clouds came scudding in and the rains began again, lashing out of an icy autumn wind. Most of the artillery could not be brought into position; the broad wooden gun platforms either sank in the mud or floated away on the rising waters. The assault troops marched most or all of the night to get to their "jump-off points," bearing sixty-pound packs, walking on duckboards—to step or slip off them meant at best a soaking, often a "bogging" from which other soldiers had to rescue the trapped man, at worst abandonment and death in the mire. It took five hours to walk a mile. Some units were on the march more than fourteen hours before being thrown immediately into the assault at daybreak. Rarely if ever in the 5000-year recorded history of warfare has a major infantry attack been launched under such appalling conditions.

No one stopped it; no one called it off. In his headquarters well behind the lines, General Haig, a man of regular habits, was enjoying a sound sleep.

At dawn October 9 the rain was as heavy as ever, artillery support was virtually nonexistent, the 30-foot-thick tangles of German barbed wire were uncut, and the attackers were simply massacred by the German machine guns. The air was so thick with machine-gun bullets over the British 146th Brigade that even the little carrier pigeons, always the best and often the only effective military communicators on the Western front, refused to fly in it.

Headlines in *the New York Times* reported this day's action: "British and French smash through wide German front north of Ypres. . .all Haig's objectives gained. . .attacks launched at dawn, with Allied airplanes cooperating effectively in a clear sky."(130) With the exception of "attacks launched at dawn," not one word of those headlines was true.

Just a month later, after the truly last assault on Passchendaele had been made, Lieutenant-General Sir Launcelot Kiggell, Chief of Staff to General Haig, finally paid a visit to the battlefront—his first of the campaign. He was riding in a car on a road that was, for the moment, still passable. As he beheld the oozing hell all around the road, even before he reached the front, he broke down and wept.

"Good God," he cried, "did we really send men to fight in *that*?"

His driver turned to him a face of stone, and spoke just five words.

"It's worse further on up."(131)

Three-quarters of a million men were killed or wounded on all sides in the Passchendaele campaign. The greatest gain was five miles.

* * * * * *

Though there is no evidence that Lenin was specifically informed about, or placed any special importance on the Passchendaele campaign in itself, he was very well aware of the kind of war World War I was, and the actual and probable consequences of such a war on the structure of society. He had seen what it had done to Russia, the gigantic opportunity it had created for him and his cause. He expected, with the same assurance he had regarding Russia, that all the other belligerents would break down as well, very soon, for many of the the same reasons. This accounts for his confidence, which reached its peak in October, that revolution would occur not only in Russia but in the whole world, which it was only necessary to control and direct, to give him and his party total victory and world dominion.

Much has been made by later commentators and critics, availing themselves of all the benefits of hindsight, of Lenin's alleged lack of realism and overconfidence regarding the Europe-wide revolution he so confidently anticipated. Inevitably, his sources of information about events outside Russia were not the best, and he should have been more conscious of the consequences of this. His euphoria was somewhat premature, even in light of what he did surely know and reasonably suspect. But he was not so far wrong as nearly everyone since has tended to think. There is good reason to believe that the Western world stood very close to final catastrophe in that ghastly autumn of 1917. How many more Passchendaeles could any nation, however disciplined and loyal to its leaders, have endured without breaking? We may presume that no inconsiderable part in preventing that ultimate collapse was played by the prayers offered for peace—by Pope Benedict XV, by the children of Fatima offering their daily rosary for peace as the Lady has asked, by the suffering and the dying, by the victims of the rural terror in Russia, and by millions more throughout Europe and the world.

Of that kind of power Lenin had no conception. Within his universe he saw victory. He sincerely believed he was about to win the world.

On September 30 he had left Helsinki for Vyborg, the last major Finnish city before the Russian frontier. His own party central committee forbade him to come to Petrograd, for he was still legally a fugitive from justice on the charges growing out of the July riots and the allegations then that he was a German spy, and for him to come to the capital city was felt to be too great a risk for him personally and for the party. Chafing angrily at this restraint, Lenin poured out from Vyborg a steady stream of communications to the party leaders in Petrograd, demanding that they strike immediately for total power. He found them very reluctant to move at once; they tended to favor waiting for the meeting of the All-Russian Congress of Soviets, scheduled for early November, which they were confident they would control, at last fulfilling Lenin's own slogan, "all power to the Soviets." But Lenin did not want—had never really wanted—the Soviets actually to take power on their own. He wanted his Communist Party to take power by itself, and then give such power as it thought desirable to the Soviets.

On October 12, in a blazing article entitled "The Crisis Is Ripe," Lenin stated his conviction that "we are on the threshold of a world proletarian revolution,"(132) and went on to review the overwhelming evidence of the breakdown of the public order in Russia: the almost complete collapse of military discipline; the unlimited revolutionary militancy of the sailors of the Baltic fleet, within cannon-shot of Petrograd; the innumerable uprisings and property seizures, amounting to revolution already in being, in the countryside. All this had opened and prepared the way for a Communist takeover. He called special attention to the results of the municipal elections just held in Moscow. The Communists had polled an absolute majority of the vote, 51 per cent, up from only 11 per cent in the municipal elections in Moscow in July; by contrast the "moderate revolutionary" parties, the Social Revolutionaries and the Mensheviks, had dropped from 70 per cent of the Moscow vote in July to only 18 per cent. The Communists were inheriting the revolution. He cited reports of military mutinies and strikes in Germany, France, Italy, and England (unfounded or minor, except for France—and that was old news—but Lenin believed these mutinies and strikes to be far more widespread than they then were, because he expected them, and because in the circumstances of the war they were logical.) To delay now, Lenin said, "would be utter idiocy or sheer treachery." It would "doom the revolution to failure."(133) If the Central Committee of his party would not act, he would resign from it and campaign for approval of his coup among the rank-and-file party members at the forthcoming party congress.

Six days later the Bolshevik Central Committee, responding to Lenin's fierce pressure, declared that it was not necessary to wait for the meeting of the All-Russian Congress of Soviets to carry out an armed uprising.

The day after Lenin wrote "The Crisis Is Ripe," the Blessed Virgin Mary made her final appearance at the Cova da Iria and performed the miracle for which her believers had been waiting, in full view of some seventy thousand people.

Many of them had been waiting all night; and all night it had rained—rain like the rain in bloody Flanders, steady, soaking, cold, falling and flying in gale of wind. (It may have been the same storm, or an offshoot, that scourged Haig's attackers October 9, three days before the pilgrims began arriving at the Cova da Iria.) Some had come astonishing distances, a hundred miles or more, from the mountains and from the coast, often with their families including the smallest children, and a burro to carry supplies for the journey. They were mostly (though not entirely) poor and humble people. They had heard that Our Lady had appeared to three of their own kind. Neither rain nor weariness could hold them back. They came, and they waited.

October 13 dawned dark gray, an image of Christian Europe that month and that year. The mothers of the three children feared terribly for them in the enormous throng. They feared even more what might happen if the Lady did not appear, and did not perform the promised miracle. Some neighbors warned the parents not to go, thinking they might be blamed and harmed if nothing happened.

But the children were unafraid, and Manuel Pedro Marto was unafraid. He kept assuring his wife and solicitous neighbors that everything was going to be all right. A neighbor carried Jacinta to the site of the apparitions, crying "Make way for the children who saw Our Lady!" as he pushed through the crowd; just behind him came Marto, holding Lucia and Francisco tightly, one by each hand. As noon came, tens of thousands of people were praying the Rosary together. The rain was still falling heavily.

Suddenly Lucia cried, "Put down your umbrellas!"—and everyone who heard her immediately did so, regardless of the continuing rain.

It was past noon. An officious priest, growing angry because Our Lady was late, concluded that she was not coming at all and tried to push the children away, shouting: "Away with all this! It is all an illusion." They stood firm.

Then Lucia saw the familiar, ineffable flash in the east. Her face flushed, and was transfigured. Jacinta and Francisco stood rapt beside her.

"Have them build a chapel here in my honor," Mary said. "I am the Lady of the Rosary. Let them continue to say the Rosary every day. The war is going to end, and the soldiers will soon return to their homes."(134)

She spoke of the necessity of sinners ceasing to offend God so much. Then she opened her lovely hands, and it seemed to Lucia that light rose straight up from them to the very zenith of the leaden sky.

The clouds parted, the sun appeared in the blue window thus opened upon the infinite, and the three children saw a tableau of the Holy Family, with Saint Joseph holding the Child Jesus on one arm. He raised the other arm three times to bless the crowd with the sign of the cross.

Then Mary appeared to Lucia as the Mother of Sorrows, with the suffering Christ of the Way of the Cross, and then as Our Lady of Mount Carmel, holding her Child.

This is what the children saw. Most of the people in the crowd saw only the sun—and what it did.

From the time it had broken through the clouds, the sun, unlike any other time they had ever seen it high in the sky, could be looked upon directly, with joy and without pain. Then it began to dance, then to whirl violently, then to fling off brilliant streamers of colored light, like a fireworks display. Then it seemed to plunge, zigzagging, toward the earth.

Thousands of people cried out and sank to the ground in terror, crying to Jesus and Mary for help.

The sun climbed back up to its normal place in the sky. Its dance, ejection of the streamers of colored light, and descent and return had occupied, altogether, about ten minutes.

It is the greatest, most abundantly recorded miracle in history since Jesus Christ walked the earth and founded His Church. Books have been filled with the testimony of the Fatima witnesses.

Only a few of the most convincing examples can be given here.

Hear Avelino da Almeida, managing editor of *O Seculo*, the largest newspaper in Lisbon, a Freemason with little use for the Catholic Church, who only that morning had written an article about the gathering at Fatima full of supercilious doubt, condescending analysis of the state of mind of the believers assembling there, and barely veiled hints of how the clergy and commercial interests were allegedly planning to profit from the apparitions.

> A spectacle unique and incredible if one had not been a witness of it . . . One can see the immense crowd turn toward the sun, which reveals itself free of the clouds in full noon. The great star of day makes one think of a silver plaque, and it is possible to look straight at it without the least discomfort. It does not burn, it does not blind. It might be like an eclipse. But now bursts forth a colossal clamor, and we hear the nearest spectators crying, "Miracle, miracle! Marvel, marvel!"
>
> Before the astonished eyes of the people, whose attitude carries us back to biblical times and who, full of terror, heads uncovered, gaze into the blue of the sky, the sun has trembled, and the sun has made some brusque movements, unprecedented and outside of all cosmic laws—the sun has "danced."(135)

Hear Dr. Domingos Pinto Coelho In *O Ordem*:

> The sun, sometimes surrounded with crimson flames, at other times aureoled with yellow and red, at still other times seemed to revolve with a very rapid movement of rotation, still again seeming to detach itself from the sky, to approach the earth and to radiate strong heat.(136)

Hear Father Inacio Lourenco, who as a boy of nine then was going to school at Alburita, more than ten miles from the Cova da Iria. He ran into the street with his teacher, Dona Delfina Pereira Lopes, to see what was happening in the sky.

> It was like a globe of snow revolving on itself. Then suddenly it seemed to come down in a zigzag, threatening to fall on the earth. Terrified, I ran to shelter myself in the midst of the people. All were weeping, expecting from one moment to the next the end of the world.
>
> Near us was an unbeliever without religion, who had spent the

morning mocking the blockheads who had made all that journey
to Fatima to go and stare at a girl. I looked at him. He stood as if
paralyzed, thunderstruck, his eyes fixed on the sun. Then I saw
him tremble from head to foot, and raising his hands to heaven,
he fell on his knees in the mire, shouting *"Nossa Senhora!
Nossa Senhora!"* [Our Lady! Our Lady!] . . .

   During those long minutes of the solar phenomenon objects all
about us reflected all the colors of the rainbow. As we looked at
one another, one seemed blue, another yellow, another
vermilion. . . . All these strange phenomena increased the terror
of the crowd. After about ten minutes the sun returned to its
place in the same way it had descended.(137)

Twenty-five miles away, the poet Afonso Lopes Vieira saw the
miracle of the sun from his own house. These distant witnesses
destroy absolutely any theory of mass suggestion or hallucination
at the Cova da Iria, generated by emotion and expectation among
the crowd there, as an explanation for what was seen in the sky.

In a world of broken promises, the Mother of God had kept her
promise. It remained to be seen how many, even yet, would hear
and heed her words and help her by their prayers, and by lives
more pleasing to God, to change the course of history—to convert
the Russia which was about to fall into Lenin's grasp.

* * * * * *

On October 16 the Bolshevik Central Committee authorized
Lenin's return to Petrograd, and a few days later he slipped back
into the city disguised by a gray wig and large spectacles, with his
beard shaved off; one observer thought he looked like a Lutheran
minister, another like an elderly music teacher. He stayed in the
fifth-floor apartment of Margarita Fofanova, an agronomy student
who worked in a publisher's office, and was not widely known to be
the militant Communist she had in fact been since the age of
nineteen. She concealed Lenin very carefully. On October 21 he
wrote a short article on the principles to be followed in making a
successful revolt. "The success of both the Russian and the world
revolution," he declared, "depends upon two or three days of
struggle."(138) On October 22 he called a crucial meeting of the

party Central Committee for the following evening. It was held in the apartment of the journalist Nikolai Sukhanov, who was not present himself. His wife acted as hostess.

One by one, twelve of the 21 members of the Central Committee of the Communist Party of Russia picked their way through the dark streets of Petrograd to Apartment 31, at 32 Karpovka Street. Name after name of that night assembly looms athwart the grim history of the twentieth century like gigantic shadows cast by a flickering fire: Lenin; Trotsky; Stalin; Kamenev and Zinoviev, Lenin's companions in exile; Sverdlov, who signed the orders that led to the murder of the Czar and his family, and gave his name to the city in the Urals where they died; Dzerzhinsky and Uritsky, the founders and organizers of the Communist secret police terror established soon after the Communist coup, never relaxed, and still existing; Sokolnikov, later Commissar of Finance and signer of the separate Russian peace treaty with Germany; Bubnov, the future Commissar of Education in Communist Russia. There were three women present: Alexandra Kollontai, the only woman member of the Central Committee, who had greeted Lenin at the Finland station in April with that lush bouquet of red roses; Varvara Yakovlieva, a "candidate member" of the Committee, who acted as secretary; and Sukhanov's wife Galina, the hostess, who served them all tea and cakes. Another "candidate member" of the Central Committee, A. Lomov, was also present.

The meeting began at ten o'clock, when Lenin arrived. It lasted more than five hours. Lenin relentlessly hammered down all questions, doubt, and indecision. Revolution now! Seize power now! Wait for nothing and no one! Set a date! "Delay is death," he kept repeating—a maxim attributed to Czar Peter the Great. Kamenev and Zinoviev, who had been his closest friends, would not give way. They knew Lenin well enough to be somewhat inured to his vehemently dominating personality; they had minds of their own, and were convinced that there was more apathy than revolutionary fervor among the Russian masses at this time. Finally, at about three o'clock in the morning, a vote was taken. It was ten to two for revolution. Only Kamenev and Zinoviev voted no.

Writing with a blunt lead pencil on a square sheet of paper torn out of a child's copy-book, Lenin scrawled the resolution the majority had approved. Following a citation of reasons for a coup, some well-grounded and some greatly distorted, the operative clause of the resolution declared: "Recognizing, therefore, that an armed uprising is inevitable and that the time is fully ripe, the C.C. proposes to all the party organizations to be guided accordingly."(139) But, despite Lenin's urgings, no date was set, and Kamenev and Zinoviev were so convinced he was wrong that they resolved to carry on the fight against this decision in larger groups of the party.

When the meeting was over, Lenin made his way back through the deserted streets, in the mists before dawn, to Fofanova's apartment. It was almost exactly the same hour that Rasputin had died at last, under the ice of the Neva, nearly ten months before.

Six days later, at another meeting of the Central Committee, this time with delegates present from the Petrograd party committee and various Communist factory committees and labor unions, held in the Petrograd suburb of Lesnoy, the decisions of October 23 were confirmed by a vote of nineteen to two after another long hammering speech by Lenin, pacing the floor with his thumbs hooked in his vest like a professor, shouting so that his harsh voice would carry over the sound of rain falling heavily on the roof. He spoke for nearly two hours. "The masses have expressed their confidence in the Bolsheviks," cried, "and they demand of us not words but deeds, a decisive policy in the struggle against war and against economic ruin." A participant tells us that his listeners hung on his words "in rapt silence, holding their breaths."(140) Kamenev and Zinoviev, still in opposition, did not pick up a single vote. The date for the rising was set for November 2, four days later.

Trotsky did not attend the October 29 meeting at Lesnoy; he was too busy with the practical planning for the rising, of which he had taken charge. Ever since the meeting of October 23 he had been going from one barracks and factory to another, summoning up all his extraordinary oratorical ability, speaking constantly and with great effect to the soldiers and workers. Most of them now felt they knew him personally; many were ready to follow him wherever he might lead. He was thrusting himself and his party in to fill the void created by the specter of anarchy. The day before the Lesnoy meeting, the representative committees of the regiments of the Petrograd garrison, meeting at Bolshevik party headquarters at the Smolny Institute, had voted no longer to obey any military movement order of Kerensky's government; on the day of the Lesnoy meeting Trotsky, speaking in the name of the "Military Revolutionary Committee" he had recently established, issued a test order to the military arsenals to distribute 5000 rifles to the civilian Red Guard set up by the Communists. His order was obeyed without question.

Now the crisis was truly ripe.

November-December 1917

Tuesday, the sixth of November, 1917. The last day of freedom and of hope in this world, for at least the greater part of a hundred years, has dawned in earth's largest country. The skies are gray, rain falling, mud everywhere; fog rolls in, pushed along by a cold wet wind from the Gulf of Finland.

On a sharp bend in the Neva River east of the Tauride Palace stands the Smolny Institute, three blocks of rigidly classical buildings under a blue and gold cupola. First intended as a convent, it was built at the beginning of the nineteenth century, in the reign of Czar Alexander I, as a school for daughters of the nobility. Close by, the five splendid domes of the Cathedral of the Resurrection rise heavenward. Smolny Institute was taken over by the Petrograd Soviet in August; it was here that the All-Russian Congress of Soviets would convene the following day, in the huge assembly hall on the second floor of the south wing, with its two rows of massive columns, great ornate chandeliers, and an empty golden frame that once held the Czar's portrait. Trotsky's Military Revolutionary Committee, which was under the auspices of the Soviet, operated out of Room 10. The Institute was now also Bolshevik headquarters; party leaders met in a small corner room on the third floor.

All night the Smolny Institute had been humming with activity. As John Reed unforgettably describes it in his classic, though vehemently pro-Communist report, *Ten Days That Shook the World*:

> The long vaulted corridors, lit by rare electric lights, were
> thronged with hurrying shapes of soldiers and workmen, some
> bent under the weight of huge bundles of newspapers,

proclamations, printed propaganda of all sorts. The sound of their heavy boots made a deep and incessant thunder on the wooden floor.(141)

At eight o'clock in the morning the Communist Party Central Committee met in the corner room on the third floor. News had come of pre-dawn government raids on party newspaper offices, of a government order to the Communist-controlled cruiser *Aurora* in the Neva to put to sea, so as to remove the menace of her guns from the city. Lenin was absent, still in hiding, as were Stalin and Zinoviev. All other members of the Central Committee were present. Sverdlov was in the chair, but Trotsky was in charge. He snapped out assignments: Dzerzhinsky, post offices and telegraph stations; Bubnov, railways; Milyutin, the food supply; Sverdlov, watch the moves of Kerensky and the Provisional Government; Kamenev (ready to assist despite his misgivings), go to work on winning over the Left Social Revolutionaries; Lomov, to Moscow to coordinate the planned rising there; military action in Petrograd to be under the command of Antonov, Podvoisky and Chudnovsky. Kamenev suggested that no member of the Central Committee leave Smolny that day; it was agreed. Twenty-four machine guns were emplaced on Smolny's roofs, and cannon in the courtyard; a company of troops was brought up, a firewood barricade built. At nine o'clock in the morning, in the name of the Military Revolutionary Committee, Trotsky issued Order Number 1 to the regimental commanders of his revolutionary militia:

> Danger threatens the Petrograd Soviet. During the night counter-revolutionary plotters attempted to call up junkers and shock battalions from the suburbs. The newspapers *Soldier* and *Worker's Road* have been closed.
> We order you to put the regiment into a state of military preparedness and to await new orders. Any delay or non-execution of the order will be regarded as treason to the Revolution.(142)

The sailors of the *Aurora* asked the Miltary Revolutionary Committee what to do; they received orders to stay where they were, in the Neva. Early in the afternoon Kerensky, completing one of his almost constant speeches, was handed Order Number 1 and read it from the podium. Uproar and near-panic followed. The rest of the afternoon was filled with confusion on both sides, for Kerensky was now too weak to be able to act decisively, and the Communists had been too hurried to make all the necessary preparations to insure that the coup would proceed smoothly.

Still in hiding in Fofanova's apartment, Lenin fretted and fumed, fearing that the opportunity toward which he had aimed his whole life might somehow at this last moment slip away. At nine-thirty in the evening he sent Fofanova to Smolny. About half an hour later he decided, be the consequences what they may, to go there himself—uninvited, unexpected, with just one companion, a young Finn named Eino Rahja. He put on his wig and tied a large handkerchief around his face, pretending to have a severe toothache. It was very dark, cold and blustery. The two men in shapeless, battered workmen's caps and coats made their way across the Liteiny Bridge over the Neva while a guard's attention was distracted. As they walked toward Smolny they were stopped by two mounted guards who demanded their passes (they had none); Rahja pretended to be drunk, and the guards rode away. Alone in the windy night with their dark destiny, the two strode on. One guard that night, arresting the totally unprotected Lenin, could perhaps have changed the whole course of history.

It was not to be. Lenin and Rahja reached Smolny untouched. For ten minutes they were unable to get in, for lack of passes. Finally they were literally pushed inside by a protesting crowd behind them. Incredible as it may seem, Lenin had never been to the Smolny Institute; he did not know where his own party offices were. While Rahja searched for Trotsky, Lenin was offered a roll and sausage by one of his Menshevik enemies, who failed to see through his workingman's disguise.

Midnight came, and with it Trotsky. It was the day of the revolution now. Trotsky told Lenin that the Communist seizure of power would begin at 2 a.m.

At that hour the Nikolayevsky and the Baltic railroad stations, with their telegraph offices, were seized by the Red Guards, along with the Tauride Palace and two ministers of the Provisional

Government. Sailors from the *Aurora* began taking control of the bridges across the Neva, which had been guarded by military cadets loyal to the government (the "junkers"). At dawn the State Bank and the central telephone exchanges were seized. A few shots were fired, but there were no casualties. Smolny Institute hummed and roared with activity; the city slept. Kerensky's calls for help to the Don Cossack regiments went unanswered. They were not interested, at this point, in taking either side; they were no friends of the Bolsheviks, but had no confidence whatever in Kerensky. All they would tell him, again and again, was that they were "getting ready to saddle their horses."(143)

The morning of November seventh broke a little grayer and a little colder than the day before. By eight o'clock Lenin knew he had won. He penned a proclamation in his sharp racing handwriting that one scholar has likened to "strings of barbed wire,"(144) announcing victory:

To the Citizens of Russia

The Provisional Government has been overthrown. State power has passed into the hands of the organ of the Petrograd Soviet, the Military Revolutionary Committee, which stands at the head of the Petrograd proletariat and garrison.

The cause for which the people have been fighting—the immediate proposal of a democratic peace, the abolition of landlord's ownership of land, workers' control over industry and the formation of a Soviet Government—this cause it assured.

Long live the workers', soldiers' and peasants' revolution!(145)

The proclamation was published at ten o'clock, read on the captured radio station, telegraphed to every province in the country, and quickly printed on handbills which were spread at once by the thousands throughout the city.

At that same hour Kerensky, despairing of help in Petrograd, left the Winter Palace, headquarters of the Provisional Government, to try to find troops at the front to defend his cause. His party rode in two cars, one borrowed from the American Embassy and still flying an American flag. Before departing, they described several large circles in the palace square while the driver of the American car tried to figure out which way to go.

At two o'clock in the afternoon Lenin and Trotsky stepped to the platform in the great assembly hall at Smolny Institute to address the now mostly Communist remaining members of the Petrograd Soviet. Trotsky's voice was bell-clear, exultant; Lenin's was cold and hoarse. But the harsh words had a terrible power.

> Comrades, the workers' and peasants' revolution, which the Bolsheviki always said must come, has been achieved. . . . Today in Russia, we must set about constructing the proletarian socialist state!(146)

The rest in anticlimax. We need not follow in detail the prolonged and farcical story of the fall of the Winter Palace, where what was left of the Provisional Government made its "last stand." It was the kind of absurd human comedy which sometimes impinges upon the greatest and most solemn events, which would be diverting if not played out on this occasion against a backdrop of illimitable tragedy: the government general who walked out on his own troops and was promptly captured by the enemy; the Communist guns in Peter and Paul Fortress which would not fire because no one had cleaned them since March; the government's machine guns which would not fire because they had no breechblocks; the defending "junkers" who were mistaken for children because they were almost children, and the defending battalion that was not mistaken for women, because they were women; the three hundred Cossacks who rode away; the telephoned cry for help from the Palace "to All, All, All" and the response of three hundred members of the non-communist Petrograd Duma who marched out "die together with the government"—for two blocks, whereupon they met a handful of Communist sailors and promptly dispersed; and the final "storming" of the huge 1500-room building during which most of the "stormers" became lost in the corridors, and the principal remaining officer among the defenders became so exhausted running up and down them that he finally collapsed in a chair saying: "I'll die here, but I can't run another step." As for the bombardment of the Winter Palace by the cruiser *Aurora*, still celebrated in Communist legend, it happened—but the shells were blanks.

The Winter Palace fell at 2 a.m. November 8. The revolution had taken exactly twenty-four hours. A handful of the revolutionaries were killed. So far as any historian has been able to determine, not a single man in Petrograd died to save Holy Mother Russia from capture by the supreme political evil of the age, the sworn enemy of God and dehumanizer of men.

It was Rasputin's ultimate legacy.

******

At 3:30 a.m. November 8 Lenin was finally prevailed upon to leave roaring Smolny and go to a nearby apartment to sleep. But he would not sleep; he stayed up all the rest of the night writing out his decree for the nationalization of all the land in Russia—the decree essentially taken from the confiscation resolutions which the Soviet of Peasants' Deputies had discussed back in June. In the morning, as Krupskaya heated the samovar for his tea, he read it to her, saying:

> What we have to do now is to proclaim and publish the decree everywhere. After this they will never get their land back again! No power on earth will be able to take back this decree from the peasants or give the land back to the land-owners. This achievement is essential for our revolution. The agrarian revolution will be accomplished and put into force today!(147)

So it was. Lenin read the decree that evening to the Congress of Soviets, to a thundering ovation, as the centerpiece for an extraordinary speech in which he called for an immediate end to the war, denouncing secret treaties and secret dipolmacy and urging on worldwide revolution. Later that night—the session of the Soviet continued until 5:15 a.m.—the Communist government was formally established under the name of Soviet of People's Commissars (Sovnarkom). Lenin was President, Trotsky Commissar for Foreign Affairs, Stalin Commissar for Nationalities.

Those observers who had not yet taken Lenin's full measure gave the new government a life expectancy of about two weeks. Most of the army did not want to fight anyone. The idea of one-party government was far from popular. The powerful railwaymen': union was wholly outside Communist influence or control. Kerensky was still at large, attempting to bring up troops from the front to regain Petrograd. The coup in Moscow at first seemed to have failed; Colonel Ryabtsev, commander of the Moscow district for the Provisional Government, an officer of real ability and resolution, at first secured and held the center of the city, including the Kremlin, despite all the revolutionaries could do. On Sunday, November 11, there was a major counter-stroke in Petrograd itself, with pitched battles around the central telephone station and at the cadet school named for King St. Vladimir, who brought Christianity to Russia. Though it was quickly overcome, Kerensky had now arrived, with a force of Cossacks under General Krasnov, at Gatchina and Tsarskoe Selo less than twenty miles from Petrograd. It was imperative for the Communists to set up defenses against them; but the troops in Petrograd refused to move. One by one the Communist military orgainzers tried and failed to persuade them. Nikolai Podvoisky came to Lenin to report failure.

"Get them out," Lenin ordered. "They must go out this very moment!"

"Krylenko has already tried and failed," Podvoisky replied, "and they wouldn't listen to me. There's absolutely nothing you can do with the regiments."

Lenin's face contorted. His narrow eyes blazed. He did not raise his voice; he did not need to. All the energy of his ferocious, world-conquering will projected from him and focussed on Podvoisky as though from a ray-gun.

"You will answer to the Central Committee if the regiments do not leave the city immediately. Do you hear me, at this very moment!"(148)

As Podvoisky tells it:

> I shot out of the room like a bullet and in a few minutes I was again at the barracks of the Volhynian Regiment. I mustered the

soldiers and said very few words to them. The soldiers must have
seen something extraordinary in my face. Silently, they rose to
their feet, and began to prepare for the campaign. And then
other regiments followed them.(149)

So did Lenin. That evening, in a heavy rain, he took personal
command of the disposition of the troops on Pulkovo Heights
outside Petrograd, though all he knew of war came form a reading
of Clausewitz while in exile in Switzerland. He demoted Antonov,
who had been the commander of the "assault" on the Winter
Palace and had managed to get himself captured earlier that day at
the telephone exchange, and put Podvoisky in command. But
Lenin was the real commander; when Podvoisky objected to his
plans, dispositions and orders being constantly overridden and
redirected, and asked to resign in consequence, Lenin snapped:
"I'll have you placed on trial before the party court and shot! Now
do your work!"(150)

Kerensky, Krasnov and the lackadaisical Cossacks had nothing
to match this. There were only about twelve hundred of them, far
from enthusiastic for their mission. After a series of skirmishes in
the rain on Pulkovo Heights November 12, Krasnov withdrew to
Gatchina. Two days later Dybenko, the huge sailor who was
another of the improbable Communist commanders, went out to
negotiate with the Cossacks. They agreed to withdraw and turn
over Kerensky in return for safe conduct to the Don and the
withdrawal of Lenin and Trotsky from the government. Dybenko
signed the agreement. Kerensky, warned just in time, fled
disguised as a sailor. (He remained in hiding in various places in
Russia for six months and then left from Murmansk, never to
return.) Back in Petrograd, it was calmly announced that Dybenko
had exceeded his instructions by negotiating on political matters.
He was given a mild reprimand, and nothing more was heard
about Lenin and Trotsky withdrawing from the government. It was
the first example of what diplomacy, Communist style, was to be
for the rest of the twentieth century.

The next day the Kremlin fell to the Communists in Moscow.

Lenin was in a state of exaltation. He worked day and night. An
apartment was set up for him and Krupskaya in the Smolny

Institute. Decree followed revolutionary decree. When the State Bank proved uncooperative, Lenin sent the State Bank Commissar to the bank with an order for ten million rubles and a detachment of Red Guards. "Don't come back without the money," Lenin said.(151) It was taken and stuffed in sacks, exactly like a bank robbery, and brought to Lenin's office. On November 22 the commander-in-chief of the Russian army, General Dukhonin, was removed by order of Lenin and replaced by Ensign Krylenko, another Bolshevik sailor. (When Krylenko took command at Mogilev eleven days later, Dukhonin was seized by his sailors and torn to pieces.) On November 27 all industry in Russia was formally taken over by the government. On December 5 an armistice was concluded at the front, which became permanent three months later by the Treaty of Brest-Litovsk with Germany. On December 6 all large houses in Russia were declared government property. On December 18 the Supreme Council of National Economy was established as a central economic planning and control agency, and divorce on demand was made law for the nation. On December 28 all owners of bank safety deposit boxes were required to open them for government inspection in three days, and all private ownership of gold was prohibited.

On November 25 the long-awaited Constituent Assembly was elected; only a quarter of the votes throughout the nation were cast for the Bolsheviks, and even in Petrograd and Moscow they had only a plurality. The peasant Social Revolutionaries had the overall majority. Consequently the Constituent Assembly was prohibited from meeting December 11, and on that day the Constitutional Democratic Party, which had a significant representation in the Assembly, was outlawed and many of its leaders were arrested. Trotsky declared, a few days later:

> We have made a modest beginning. We have arrested the chiefs of the Cadets [Constitutional Democrats] and ordered that a watch be kept on their followers in the provinces. At the time of the French Revolution, the Jacobins guillotined men more honest than these for obstructing the people's will.(152)

On December 26 Lenin declared in *Pravda* that the only action by the Constituent Assembly that he would accept, when it finally did convene in January, was its unconditional recognition and ratification of his government and all that it had done.

Forces of opposition were gathering. Generals Kornilov and Denikin escaped from the Mogilev area just 36 hours before Krylenko and his murderous sailors arrived, and made their way to the Don where Ataman Kaledin was at last rallying the Cossacks for a real fight. And on Lenin's own revolutionary side, in the second of a series of thundering articles in the periodical *New Life*, the widely respected old socialist Maxim Gorky not only scathingly repudiated Lenin and all his works, but laid bare some of the deepest wellsprings of his character and purposes:

> It does not worry Lenin in the least that Russia must suffer this tragedy: he is the slave of dogma, and his followers are his slaves. He has no knowledge of life in all its complex variety; he does not know the masses; he has not lived with them. But he has learned from books how they can be made to revolt, and—what is much easier—how their instincts can be aroused. For the Leninist the working class is like a mineral in the hands of the metallurgist. . . .
>
> He spends his time like a chemist in the laboratory, but with this difference—the chemist works on inert matter and produces results which are helpful to life, while Lenin works on living flesh and drags the revolution to its doom.(153)

The answer to Kornilov, Denikin and Kaledin on the right, to the Constitutional Democrats in the center, to Gorky and the Social Revolutionaries on the left, was in every case the same: terror.

On December 20 Lenin created, for this purpose, one of the most feared organizations the world has ever known—so much feared, so much hated, that its name has been changed, for propaganda purposes and to divert attention from it, no less than five times since its founding; but the reality has remained the same. It began as the All-Russian Extraordinary Commission for Struggle against Counter-Revolution and Sabotage—CHEKA. Then it became OGPU, then NKVD, then MVD; now it is KGB. So it was born; it needed a head.

"Where are we going to find our Fouquier-Tinville?" Lenin asked.(154) Fouquier-Tinville was the public prosecutor of the French Revolution, during the Reign of Terror, who sent at least a hundred men and women to the guillotine every day.

Lenin's choice was Felix Dzerzhinsky, the Polish Communist who had been at the epochal meeting in Sukhanov's apartment October 23 where it was decided to make the Communist Revolution. He would be assisted by another participant in that meeting, Moses Uritsky.

At some time during these final weeks of 1917, the first of his revolutionary government, Lenin was visited at the Smolny Institute by a very old friend, from out of a past that must then have seemed to him as distant as a dream: Georgy Solomon, who had known him as a 22-year-old student in Samara on the Volga, a full quarter of a century ago, and had not seen him for ten years. They had a long talk. Solomon's account of it is the most revealing glimpse we have of the mind and heart and soul of Lenin the triumphant revolutionary:

> We are . . . the real revolutionaries—yes, we are going to tear the whole thing down! We shall destroy and smash everything, ha-ha-ha, with the result that everything will be smashed to smithereens and fly off in all directions, and nothing will remain standing!
>
> Yes, we are going to destroy everything, and on the ruins we will build our temple! It will be a temple for the happiness of all! But we shall destroy the entire bourgeoisie, and grind them to powder—ha-ha-ha—to powder. Remember that! . . .
>
> And remember that the Lenin who talked to you ten years ago no longer has any existence. He died a long time ago. In his place there speaks the new Lenin, who has learned that the ultimate truth lies in communism, which must now be brought into existence. It may not please you, and you may think it is nothing but utopian adventurism, but I assure you it isn't. . . .
>
> And don't talk to me. It will be better for you if you don't talk, for I shall attack mercilessly anyone who smells of counter-revolution. Against the counterrevolutionaries, whoever they are, I shall employ Comrade Uritsky, ha-ha-ha. Do you know him? It will be better for you, I think, if you don't make his acquaintance.(155)

Georgy Solomon went away. He had come to see the friend of his youth—and he had looked into the face of Hell.

Road To Judgment: 1918-1924

The barren victory of the Entente powers in World War I was won November 11, 1918 and sealed by the dictated peace of Versailles June 28, 1919. The thrones of Imperial Germany and Imperial Austria were toppled, Kaiser Wilhelm and Emperor Charles exiled. The Austro-Hungarian Empire was destroyed, leaving only a tiny rump republic in the mountains—modern Austria. Woodrow Wilson collapsed in Pueblo, Colorado in September 1919 and lay between life and death for months, overcome by his own desperate struggle to convince the American people that after all their sons had died for something worthwhile in the war: his vision of the League of Nations as an international peace-keeping authority, which the United States would not accept. Pope Benedict XV lived until 1922; the shadow of the gigantic catastrophe he had witnessed never left his thin face. As for Lenin, for four harrowing, hammering years—1918, 1919, 1920, 1921—he held his revolutionary regime together against a host of enemies foreign and domestic, from his own Kronstadt sailors who rose against him in 1921 to British and French tanks spearheading the White armies of Denikin which at one point pushed more than halfway from the Don the Moscow. In the end he defeated them all; his titanic will prevailed. He grew wan and haggard, tortured by headaches, debilitated by insomnia; his face in those four years shows a fearful hardening and aging. But still he ruled; and although there had been no world revolution, there was now a large, indubitably effective, well-organized and well-financed world revolutionary movement: the Communist International.

Upon the stricken world of 1919 the great influenza epidemic fell, the worst in centuries, the killer of the young and the apparently strong. In April it took Francisco Marto to be with his Lady forever.

"Goodbye, Francisco, till Heaven," Lucia said to him as she left him for the last time on April 3, with tears streaming down her face.

Jacinta had been stricken as well. Eventually the influenza left her, but its ravages brought on purulent pleurisy—an infection of the chest which, in those days before antibiotics, took months to heal, and sometimes never healed. She was taken to the hospital in Ourem; there the doctors made an incision in her chest to drain out the pus, but she did not improve. The infection remained, and the incision remained open. In August she was brought home, weak and emaciated. In the fall she improved slightly, enough to go to Mass in Fatima and even to the Cova da Iria. Then she relapsed, and was in constant pain, which she offered up for sinners, developing a fully understood vocation of suffering. In December 1919 she felt that Mary spoke to her, telling her that she would soon go to a hospital in Lisbon, and there she would die—alone. But Mary repeated her promise that Jacinta would join her in Heaven. The next month, January 1920, Reverend Doctor Manuel Nunes Formigao, canon of the Lisbon Cathedral and professor at Santarem Seminary, who had begun investigating the Fatima apparitions and the children in September 1917 and had become one of their most convinced champions, came to take Jacinta to Lisbon for the best medical treatment Portugal could offer. Before leaving, she rode on a burro to the Cova da Iria for a last visit. She prayed the Rosary there, as the Queen of Heaven had asked on that bright May day three years before, and she picked flowers to place as an offering in the chapel that had been built by the faithful near the tree of the apparitions.

To Lucia the next morning she said:

> We shall never meet again. Pray for me a lot till I go to Heaven, and afterwards I'll pray a lot for you. Never tell anybody the secret even if they kill you. Love Jesus and the Immaculate Heart of Mary a great deal and make many sacrifices for sinners.(156)

Jacinta was not quite ten years old.

On February 10 she was operated on in the Hospital of Dona Stefania in Lisbon. The surgeons made a huge opening in her chest. It did not help. For six days she lay in excruciating pain. Then the pain left her. On February 20 she was anointed. At ten-thirty that evening she died, a rosy flush on her cheeks, a smile on her lips. On February 23 she was buried at Ourem. A gentle fragrance hung about her casket. Long ago in the Christian centuries, it had been called the odor of sanctity.

* * * * * *

Charles, Emperor of Austria and Apostolic King of Hungary, heir of the Holy Roman Empire, had firmly refused either to abdicate or to cling to power. He had voluntarily withdrawn from government in the hopeless final days of defeat in the autumn of 1918; he stood ready to return whenever his people needed and wanted him again. To Hungary, after the nightmare rule of the Communist Bela Kun in 1919 and a miserable succession of foreign occupations and governments whose terms of office were measured in weeks or days, he made two attempts to return in 1921. Both were frustrated by the treachery of Admiral Nicholas Horthy, who had claimed to be preparing the way as regent for his restoration, but actually wanted—and finally obtained—the rule for himself. Generally condemned in consequence of these actions as a disturber of the peace, Charles—the only sovereign of the powers engaged in the First World War who had conscientiously sought peace—was banished to the Portuguese island of Madeira, without any source of income. The government of the new Austrian republic conficated all of his property in Austria. The Habsburg family jewels had been brought to Zurich and left there with an Austrian lawyer named Bruno Steiner, who sold them and disappeared with the proceeds. Forced by lack of funds to move at the beginning of March 1922 to a house in the damp, ever-misty mountains over Funchal in Madeira, with only smoky green wood to burn for warmth, Charles—never physically strong—caught a cold which rapidly developed into pneumonia. On March 25 he had a raging fever; the doctors could not help him. Zita almost never left his bedside. On March 27 he was anointed; still holding a crucifix, he called his ten-year-old son Otto to his side. Of their conversation he said only: "I had to call him to show him an example. He has to learn how one conducts oneself in such situations—as Catholic and as Emperor."(157)

As Catholic first . . . A priest, Father Zsamboki, was in the house all during Charles' last days, saying Mass, giving him communion. Charles declared: "I forgive all my enemies, all who have made me suffer, and all who have worked against me."(158) As death approached Charles prayed, hour after hour, with Zita's hand in his. Often the prayer they said together was the Rosary.

Madeira was Portuguese territory, Fatima not so very far away. Had Charles and Zita heard of Our Lady's coming there? We do not know.

On March 31, 1922 Charles' mind began to wander, to reach out toward the beloved land he had lost. He said to Zita: "Why don't they let us go home? I long so much to go home with you. . . Let's go home together—we are already so near."(159) At another time he said, calmly and clearly: "I must suffer like this so that my people can come together again."(160) When, on the morning of April 1, it became very difficult for him to speak, Zita said prayers for them both softly, against his ear. Just before noon he looked up at her and whispered: "I love you so much." Then he asked for a last communion, caressed a crucifix, murmured "Thy will be done," and died with the name of Jesus on his lips.(161)

* * * * * *

On May 26, 1922—less than two months after Charles' death—Lenin had his first stroke.

He was just fifty-two years old, and before taking power in Russia had always enjoyed excellent health. But for him as for his victims, the revolutionary Utopia was proving to be a death trap. The frequent severe headaches had been a warning he had not heeded. The first stroke was relatively mild, but it interfered with his coordination on the right side and slurred his speech. He knew what it was. One day he challenged Dr. Mikhail Auerbach about it directly.

"They say you are a brave man," Lenin said to him. "Tell me the truth. Is it paralysis, and is it getting worse? . . . If it is paralysis, of what use would I be, and who would have need of me?"(162)

Dr. Auerbach did not know what to answer.

The doctors urged Lenin to rest, to avoid the pressures and tensions of news and politics. To some extent he obeyed them, and gradually improved. After four months he returned to work, but on a greatly reduced schedule. Studying the plans for establishing the Union of Soviet Socialist Republics (U.S.S.R.), he began to discover that the Commissar for Nationalities was in the process concentrating all power in the non-Russian regions of the Soviet Union into his hands. Since the Commissar for Nationalities was also Commissar of the Inspectorate (the watchdog of the whole Communist governmental structure) and General Secretary of the Central Committee of the Communist Party, this caused Lenin some uneasiness, even though he had appointed the man to all three posts. He was Joseph Stalin, the "man who got things done," the bank robber of the Caucasus, the fisherman of the death-cold Yenisei, the "gray blur" of the revolution, who now began to stalk Lenin exactly like one of the great gray man-eating wolves of the winter-bound Siberian *taiga.*

Already Stalin was the most powerful man in the Communist government next to Lenin himself. He visited Lenin four times between the day of his stroke and August 19, taking the measure of his physical and mental debilitation. On September 26 Lenin criticized Stalin's policy on non-Russian nationalities in a letter to the Politburo. Stalin replied at once, stating flatly that Lenin's suggested changes were "hurried" and "should not be adopted."(163) Returning to work October 2, overwhelmed with more problems than he could handle on his reduced schedule, Lenin did not immediately react to this revealingly impudent defiance.

On December 12 he was visited by Felix Dzerzhinsky, the gaunt and saturnine Pole whom he had chosen as the executioner

of the Russian revolution, its "Fouquier-Tinville," the head of the
secret police. Discussing the nationalities question with
Dzerzhinsky, Lenin realized that he was now hand in glove with
Stalin. Lenin began to sense growing, creeping danger. The next
day he met with Stalin for more than two hours. What they said to
each other has never been revealed.

Three days later, December 16, 1922, Lenin had his second
stroke. There was a more extended paralysis of his right side. He
was ghost-pale, unable to stand, but he could still speak—though
he knew he might lose the power of speech at any moment. He was
attended, in the Kremlin apartment where he lay, by Krupskaya,
his devoted secretary Fotieva, other secretaries whom he could
trust, and one whom his could not—for she was Stalin's wife. On
December 18 she was dismissed, probably by Krupskaya, since
Lenin was then incapacitated.

On December 21 Lenin whispered to Krupskaya a message for
Trotsky, who replied by a telephone which Stalin had tapped,
thereby revealing to Stalin that Lenin and Trotsky were beginning
to collaborate specifically against him. The next day Stalin struck
at Krupskaya. He telephoned her, loosed a torrent of obscene
abuse, ordered her to stay out of politics, and threatened her with
a party trial. It seems that she did not immediately tell Lenin about
this call, but in any case he knew very well what was now at stake.
The revolution was about to devour not only its children, but its
father. On December 24 Stalin met with the Politburo and the
doctors attending Lenin. He was to be allowed no visitors and no
incoming letters. Only Krupskaya and his secretaries (except for
the doctors) would have access to him.

From the very gates of Hell, Lenin fought back. His
indomitable will never faltered. All during the day his isolation
was decreed, he suffered violent headaches. Nevertheless, that
evening, he called in his secretary Maria Volodicheva and dictated
to her the continuation of a message he had been preparing to the
Twelfth Congress of the Rusian Communist Party, scheduled to
meet in the spring:

> Comrade Stalin, having become General Secretary, has
> concentrated immeasurable power in his hands, and I am not

sure that he always knows how to use that power with sufficient caution. On the other hand Comrade Trotsky . . . is distinguished not only by his exceptional abilities—personally, to be sure, he is perhaps the most able man in the present Central Committee—but also by his exceptional self-assurance and exceptional enthusiasm.(164)

After warning Maria Volodicheva on no account to mention this to anyone, he sealed the document in an envelope on which he told her to write: "To be opened only by V. I. Lenin, or in the event of his death by Nadezhda Konstantinovna [Krupskaya]."(165)

On January 4, 1923 Lenin added a postscript, the "bombshell" of his "last testament." It is likely that by then Krupskaya had told him of Stalin's attack on her.

> Stalin is too coarse, and this fault, though tolerable in dealings among us Communists, becomes unbearable in a General Secretary. Therefore I propose to the comrades to find some way of removing Stalin from his position and appointing somebody else who differs in all respects from Comrade Stalin in one characteristic—namely, someone more tolerant, more loyal, more polite and considerate to his comrades.(166)

It was very late in the day for Lenin to be pleading for tolerance, politeness and consideration—qualities he had never shown himself in his dealings with the world—and he got none. But he continued to fight relentlessly against his disease, rallying more quickly than the doctors had thought possible. All through February he was gaining strength. The party congress would open March 30. He even hoped he might be able to address it in person. If he did, he could dispose of Stalin. On March 5 he demanded an apology from Stalin for his treatment of Krupskaya, failing which he would sever all relations with him, and appealed directly to Trotsky for help in bringing charges against Stalin before the upcoming party congress, based on his atrocities in Georgia. On March 7 Trotsky replied that he dared not act against Stalin without the support of Kamenev, who was acting chairman of the Party Central Committee in the absence of Lenin, the chairman. Lenin had never really trusted Kamenev since he voted against the revolution at that decisive meeting at Sukhanov's apartment in Petrograd October 22, 1917.

"Kamenev will immediately show everything to Stalin," Lenin said to Fotieva when she reported Trotsky's reply, "and then Stalin will make a rotten compromise and deceive everyone."(167)

Still Trotsky could not be persuaded to move alone, and Lenin had to yield to his insistence. Lenin saw his power dissolving before his eyes, his last combination to retain it compromised. His condition worsened; his words began to come with difficulty. Handing Fotieva the note which permitted Kamenev to be told as Trotsky had demanded, he muttered: "Before it is too late. . .I am obliged to come out openly before the proper time."(168)

On March 9, 1923 Lenin had his third stroke, which completely paralyzed his right side, partially paralyzed the rest of his body, and took away entirely his power of speech.

For two weeks his doctors expected him to die at any moment. He could not speak, he could not move, he could not sleep. With eyes open and staring at the ceiling, he fought on with unconquerable tenacity, day after day. He clung to life; then, astonishingly, he began to rally once again. Stalin, who had thought the battle won, now could not be sure. By July Lenin could walk a little, and sleep again. By September he could climb stairs; the paralysis in his left side was gone; he could understand perfectly when spoken to, and respond with a few simple words. In October he even made a visit to his Kremlin office.

Meanwhile Fotieva, a woman of remarkable courage, had on her own authority conveyed additional material prepared by Lenin and highly critical of Stalin, to Trotsky and Kamenev. Stalin was able to prevent its publication only by alleging that Lenin had not put it into final form before his third stroke, and by bullying Trotsky into temporary silence. But the charges lay in the party files like a time bomb. If Lenin recovered, they could be revived. Meanwhile Stalin and Dzerzhinsky dominated the Twelfth Communist Party Congress, constantly quoting Lenin in such a way as to support what they were doing. Stalin's opponents were reduced to meeting in the Cave of the Dead Mule near Kislovodsk to try to find a way of stopping him. No way appeared.

Only Lenin's life stood between Joseph Vissarionovich Djugashvili called Stalin, and supreme power in the largest country in the world, the capital of the Communist revolution.

Lenin was living at the Morozov palace in Gorki 23 miles from Moscow, on a forested hilltop, white and still in the Russian winter. A contingent of doctors was more or less constantly in attendance, along with Dzerzhinsky's secret police agents disguised as gardeners, woodcutters, launderers, cooks, and male nurses. Disguises did not deceive Lenin, himself a master of disguise; his mind was now working at almost full efficiency, with the terrible exception of his inability to speak more than a few words. Some of his doctors he seemed to enjoy; others he hated and feared. Steadily he improved. At the rate of three or four words a day, he was relearning language. Dr. Auerbach, who had been attending him from the beginning of his illness, was amazed at his progress.

From January 16 to January 18, 1924, at the Thirteenth Congress of the Communist Party of the Soviet Union, Stalin established his full power over the party and the country. He denounced Trotsky (who was not there, due to illness of his own) for no less than six major errors, principally for doing what Stalin himself had in fact already done, "elevating himself into a superior standing above the Central Committee, above its laws, and above its decisions."(169) Stalin threatened the absent Trotsky with expulsion from the party, and brutally suppressed all speakers who tried to oppose his will.

On the morning of January 19 Krupskaya read Lenin the full account of the party congress proceedings in *Pravda*. She reports: "He was very disturbed."(170) That afternoon she took him on a sleigh ride; that evening she read him Jack London's grim story "Love of Life"—a tale of a man abandoned in the Arctic wilderness, lost, starving, but refusing to surrender to his fate, followed by a sick wolf which eventually he kills with his bare hands, and drinks its blood. Krupskaya says Lenin was "extraordinarily pleased "(171) with the story. We can guess why.

Two days later Lenin awoke in good health; but during the morning there was a stream of telephone calls from officials in the government and the secret police, all inquiring with some urgency about his condition. The telephone was ringing almost constantly.

During the afternoon Lenin dozed. At six o'clock he began breathing with difficulty. Convulsions followed, and at 6:50 p.m. the doctors pronounced him dead.

Eleven years later, in one of Stalin's prisons, a woman named Elizabeth Lermolo, who survived to write a book, met an old Bolshevik named Gavril Volkov, who did not. He told her he had been a cook for Lenin at Gorki at the time he died. He said that on January 21, 1924 he had entered Lenin's room at eleven o'clock in the morning to bring him a "second breakfast." Lenin tried to get up, tried to speak, but could do neither. Then he put a note in Volkov's hands, just before the doctor hurried in to give Lenin an injection.

The note read: "Gavrilushka, I've been poisoned . . . go fetch Nadya [Krupskaya] at once . . . tell Trotsky . . . tell everyone you can."(172)

Volkov had been too frightened to tell anyone. But after the passage of more than fifty years, enough additional circumstantial evidence has emerged to make his report seem very likely to be true. Lenin had been killed by his own executioners. The evidence indicates that the decision to kill Lenin was probably made about the time of the opening of the Thirteenth Party Congress, where Stalin was to dispose of all his other opponents; that some of Lenin's doctors were suborned; and that the secret police were expecting his death January 21. The autopsy on Lenin was delayed, distorted, and contains obvious falsehoods.

Helpless, speechless, alone, betrayed and probably poisoned by his "comrades" of the revolution, Vladimir Ilyich Ulyanov called Lenin, the maker of the Communist revolution, died in agony and terror, his body racked by convulsions so violent that at times they flung it up into the air.

For five days, from January 23 to January 27, his body lay in state in Moscow's Hall of Columns in the House of Trade Unions, under a blood-red blanket, in a blood-red coffin. All four days snow fell incessantly. The temperature was twenty degrees below zero. Then the coffin was laid in a vault beneath the Kremlin wall, borne by eight men. One of them was Stalin, in all probability his murderer.

* * * * * *

A contest that embraces Heaven, Earth, and Hell does not end in the grave. Even the dead fight on. So the cosmic Battle of 1917 continues to echo through time and space, into the realms beyond mortality.

In 1935 the body of Jacinta was taken from the cemetery at Ourem. Her face was untouched, incorrupt;(173) there was still the sweet fragrance that had enfolded her at burial fifteen years before. She was reburied in a common grave with Francisco, of whom only bones remained.

In 1972, after the first steps in the Catholic Church's long process of beatification had been taken in the case of Emperor Charles of Austria, his tomb on Madeira was opened—fifty years after his death—in the presence of his son Otto, the Bishop of Feldkirch in Austria, the Bishop of Funchal in Madeira, and many others. Charles' body was found almost completely incorrupt.(174) The tomb was closed; the proceedings continued. For Catholics, an incorrupt body is a possible sign—no more—of beatitude.

In 1974, the body of Arturo da Oliveira Santos, once the Adminstrator of Ourem, who had threatened the Fatima children with boiling oil and prevented them by incarceration from seeing the Blessed Virgin Mary on August 13, 1917—who had died decades before, unrepentant, and therefore refused burial in consecrated ground by the Catholic Church—was, by order of a pro-Communist government then briefly in power, exhumed and reburied in consecrated ground.

For four and a half months after Lenin's body was placed in the vault beneath the Kremlin wall, a team of doctors worked to embalm it so well that it would be preserved "for a thousand years." But the embalming was a failure. When the vault was opened in the summer of 1924, its shrunken face was gray and wrinkled, like that of a man who had died at a great age. In 1926 it suddenly looked younger; the government let it be said that one Dr. Ilya Zbarsky had discovered a new embalming process, improving on that of the ancient Egyptians, which apparently not only preserved corpses but brightened their appearance. In 1930 the present immense tomb of red granite and porphyry was opened; in it Lenin's face, under a glaring orange light, looked younger still. That tomb still stands in Red Square, the center of the Communist world, the focal point of all its most splended and bellicose ceremonies, dominated by the presence of that body—or whatever is left of it. The tomb and the body will remain there, in all probability, until Russia is converted, as the Mother of God promised at Fatima, ushering in a new age in the history of the world and of Christendom.

Endnotes

1 Gordon Brook-Shepherd, *The Last Habsburg* (London, 1968), p. 46, quoting the recollections of Empress Zita.
2 David Lloyd George, *War Memoirs* (Boston, 1934), IV, 320-321.
3 Bernard Pares, *The Fall of the Russian Monarchy* (New York, 1939, 1961), p. 143.
4 *Ibid.*, p. 145, quoting the monk Illiodor.
5 Robert K. Massie, *Nicholas and Alexandra* (New York, 1967), pp. 210-211.
6 *Ibid.*, p. 209.
7 *Ibid.*, p. 317.
8 Pares, *Fall of the Russian Monarchy*, p. 146.
9 *Ibid.*, p. 317.
10 *Ibid.*, p. 318.
11 *Ibid.*, p. 394.
12 *Ibid.*, pp. 394-395.
13 *Ibid.*, p. 397
14 *Ibid.*, p. 398.
15 Harrison Salisbury, *Black Night, White Snow: Russia's Revolutions, 1905-1917* (New York, 1978), pp. 261-262.
16 Robert Payne, *The Life and Death of Lenin* (New York, 1964), p. 252, quoting a letter from Lenin to Inessa Armand.
17 William Thomas Walsh, *Our Lady of Fatima* (New York, 1947, 1954), p. 17.
18 Matthew 19:14.
19 Walsh, *Our Lady of Fatima*, p. 36.
20 *Ibid.*, pp. 36-37.
21 Brook-Shepherd, *The Last Habsburg*, p. 54.
22 *Ibid.*, pp. 54-55.
23 Pares, *Fall of the Russian Monarchy*, p. 399.
24 Felix Youssoupoff, *Rasputin: His Malignant Influence and His Assassination* (London, 1927, 1934), p. 162.
25 *Ibid.*, pp. 162-163.
26 *Ibid.*, p. 168.
27 Salisbury, *Black Night, White Snow*, p. 305.
28 *Ibid.*

29 *Ibid.*
30 Richard S. Luckett, *The White Generals* (London, 1971), p. 27.
31 Barbara Tuchman, *The Zimmermann Telegram* (New York, 1958, 1966), p. 134.
32 Gerhard Ritter, *The Sword and the Scepter,* Volume III (Coral Gables, Fla., 1972), p. 314.
33 Arthur S. Link, *Wilson: Campaigns for Progressivism and Peace, 1916-1917* (Princeton, N.J., 1965), p. 147.
34 Tuchmann, *Zimmermann Telegram,* p. 137.
35 Brook-Shepherd, *The Last Habsburg,* p. 77.
36 *Ibid.,* p. 77n (quoting recollections of Empress Zita).
37 Link, *Wilson: Campaigns for Progressivism and Peace,* pp. 265-266.
38 *Ibid.,* p. 271.
39 G. de Manteyer, ed. *Austria's Peace Offer, 1916-1917* (London, 1921), p. 39, quoting memorandum from Prince Sixte de Bourbon-Parma to President Poincare of France, March 5, 1917.
40 *Ibid.,* p. 53 (note from Charles to Entente powers).
41 Salisbury, *Black Night, White Snow,* p. 335.
42 *Ibid.,* 337.
43 *Ibid.,* p. 339.
44 *Ibid.,* p. 347.
45 Pares, *Fall of the Russian Monarchy,* pp. 424-425.
46 Salisbury, *Black Night, White Snow,* p. 51.
47 *Ibid.,* p. 351n.
48 *Ibid.,* p. 355.
49 Alexander Kerensky, *Russia and History's Turning Point* (New York, 1965), p. 194.
50 Pares, *Fall of the Russian Monarchy,* p. 449.
51 Massie, *Nicholas and Alexandra,* p. 405.
52 de Manteyer, *Austria's Peace Offer 1916-1917,* p. 70.
53 *Ibid.,* p. 71.
54 *Ibid.,* p. 72.
55 *Ibid.,* p. 73.
56 *Ibid.,* p. 74.
57 *Ibid.,* p. 76.
58 *Ibid.*
59 *Ibid.,* p. 79.
60 *Ibid.,* p. 84.
61 Walter Millis, *Road to War, America 1914-1917* (Boston, 1935), p. 429.
62 *Ibid.,* p. 430.
63 Link, *Wilson: Campaigns for Progressivism and Peace,* pp. 425-426.
64 Andre Maurois, *Lyautey* (New York, 1931), p. 304.
65 Leon Wolff, *In Flanders Fields, the 1917 Campaign* (New York, 1958) p. 63.

66   Jere C. King, *Generals and Politicans; Conflict between France's High Command, Parliament and Government, 1914-1918* (Berkeley, Ca., 1951), p. 154.
67   Brook-Shepherd, *The Last Habsburg*, p. 78.
68   *Ibid.*, p. 103.
69   *Ibid.*
70   Payne, *Lenin*, p. 296.
71   *Ibid.*, p. 303.
72   Robert Payne, *The Rise and Fall of Stalin* (New York, 1965), p. 187.
73   Payne, *Lenin*, p. 311.
74   *Ibid.*, pp. 311, 312.
75   *Ibid.*, p. 318.
76   *Ibid.*, pp. 319-320, 325-326.
77   Payne, *Stalin*, p. 177.
78   *Ibid.*, p. 198.
79   *Ibid.*, p. 19.
80   King, *Generals and Politicans*, p. 140.
81   Richard M. Watt, *Dare Call It Treason: the French Army Mutinies, 1917* (New York, 1963), p. 176.
82   Quoted in John Ellis, *Eye-Deep in Hell; Trench Warfare in World War I* (New York, 1976), p. 9.
83   Walter H. Peters, *The Life of Benedict XV* (Milwaukee, 1959), p. 89.
84   *Ibid.*, p. 103.
85   *Ibid.*, p. 117.
86   *Ibid.*, p. 119.
87   *Ibid.*, p. 123.
88   Henry E.G. Rope, *Benedict, the Pope of Peace* (London, 1941), pp. 104-105.
89   *Ibid.*, pp. 122-123.
90   Walsh, *Our Lady of Fatima*, p. 49.
91   *Ibid.*, p. 51.
92   *Ibid.*, pp. 51-52.
93   *Ibid.*, p. 52.
94   *Ibid.*, p. 56.
95   Luckett, *White Generals*, p. 53.
96   de Manteyer, *Austria's Peace Offer, 1916-1917*, p. 165n.
97   Walsh, *Our Lady of Fatima*, p. 68.
98   Wolff, *In Flanders Fields*. p. 107.
99   *Ibid.*
100   Lloyd George, *War Memoirs*, IV, 397.
101   Wolff, *In Flanders Fields*, p. 113.
102   Walsh, *Our Lady of Fatima*, pp. 79-80.
103   *Ibid.*, p. 81.
104   G. K. Chesterton, "Letpanto."

105 Walsh, *Our Lady of Fatima*, pp. 81-82.
106 *Ibid.*, p. 82.
107 *Ibid.*
108 Salisbury, *Black Night, White Snow*, p. 442.
109 William H. Chamberlin, *The Russian Revolution* (New York, 1935, 1965), I, 178.
110 Walsh, *Our Lady of Fatima*, p. 115.
111 Lloyd George, *War Memoirs*, IV, 278.
112 Peters, *Benedict XV*, pp. 148-149.
113 *Ibid.*, pp. 149-151.
114 Wolff, *In Flanders Fields*, p. 149.
115 Salisbury, *Black Night, White Snow*, p. 425.
116 Chamberlin, *Russian Revolution*, I, 248.
117 *Ibid.*, p. 199.
118 *Ibid.*, p. 197.
119 Luckett, *The White Generals*, p. 80.
120 Chamberlin, *Russian Revolution*, I, 217.
121 Walsh, *Our Lady of Fatima*, p. 127.
122 *Ibid.*
123 Chamberlin, *Russian Revolution*, I, 288.
124 Payne, *Lenin*, pp. 356-357.
125 Wolff, *In Flanders Fields*, p. 178.
126 *Ibid.*, p. 181.
127 *Ibid.*, p. 184.
128 *Ibid.*, p. 185.
129 *Ibid.*, p. 187.
130 *Ibid.*, p. 205.
131 *Ibid.*, p. 228.
132 Chamberlin, *Russian Revolution*, I, 288.
133 Salisbury, *Black Night, White Snow*, p. 460.
134 Walsh, *Our Lady of Fatima*, p.144.
135 *Ibid.*, p. 147.
136 *Ibid.*, p. 148.
137 *Ibid.*, p. 149.
138 Payne, *Lenin*, p. 363.
139 *Ibid.*, p. 369.
140 Payne, *Stalin*, p. 224.
141 John Reed, *Ten Days That Shook the World* (New York, 1919), pp. 87-88.
142 Chamberlin, *Russian Revolution*, I, 309.
143 *Ibid.*, p. 313.
144 Payne, *Lenin*, p. 399.
145 *Ibid.*, p. 386.
146 Chamberlin, *Russian Revolution*, I, 316; Payne, *Lenin*, p. 389.

147   Payne, *Lenin*, p. 396.
148   *Ibid.*, p. 403.
149   *Ibid.*, p. 404.
150   *Ibid.*, p. 405.
151   Salisbury, *Black Night, White Snow*, p. 544.
152   Isaac Deutscher, *The Prophet Armed; Trotsky: 1879-1921* (New York, 1954), p. 338.
153   Payne, *Lenin*, p. 409.
154   Salisbury, *Black Night, White Snow*, p. 545.
155   Payne, *Lenin*, pp. 419-420.
156   Walsh, *Our Lady of Fatima*, p. 177.
157   Brook-Shepherd, *The Last Habsburg*, p. 328.
158   Ernst Joseph Gorlich, *Der letzet Kaiser—ein Heiliger?* (Stein am Rheim, 1972), p. 114.
159   Brook-Shepherd, *The Last Habsburg*, p. 330.
160   Gorlich, *Die letzte Kaiser*, p. 146.
161   *Ibid.*; Brook-Shepherd, *The Last Habsburg*, p. 330.
162   Payne, *Lenin*, p. 552.
163   Payne, *Stalin*, pp. 317-318.
164   Payne, *Lenin*, pp. 564-565.
165   *Ibid.*, p. 566.
166   *Ibid.*, p. 571.
167   *Ibid.*, p. 578.
168   *Ibid.*, p. 579.
169   *Ibid.*, p. 590.
170   Payne, *Stalin*, p. 365.
171   *Ibid.*, p. 367.
172   Payne, *Lenin*, p. 603.
173   Walsh, *Our Lady of Fatima*, p. 217.
174   Gorlich, *Die letzte Kaiser*, pp. 154-156.

Bibliography

Brook-Shepherd, Gordon, *The Last Habsburg* (London, 1968)
Carr, E. H., *The Bolshevik Revolution, 1917-1923*, Volumes I and II (New York, 1950-52)
Chamberlin, William H., *The Russian Revolution*, Volume I, 1917-1918: "From the Overthrow of the Czar to the Assumption of Power by the Bolsheviks" (New York, 1935, 1965)
Deutscher, Isaac, *The Prophet Armed; Trotsky: 1879-1921* (New York, 1954)
Ellis, John, *Eye-Deep in Hell; Trench Warfare in World War I* (New York, 1976)
Gorlich, Ernst Joseph, *Der letzte Kaiser—ein Heiliger?; Kaiser Karl von Osterreich* (Stein am Rhein, 1972)
Kerensky, Alexander F., *Russia and History's Turning Point* (New York, 1965)
King, Jere C., *Generals and Politicians: Conflict between France's High Command, Parliament and Government, 1914-1918* (Berkeley, Ca., 1951)
Lehovich, Dimitry, *White Against Red; the Life of General Anton Denikin* (New York, 1974)
Link, Arthur S., *Wilson: Campaigns for Progressivism and Peace, 1916-1917* (Princeton, N.J., 1965)
Lloyd George, David, *War Memoirs*, Volume IV: 1917 (Boston, 1934)
Luckett, Richard S., *The White Generals* (London, 1971)
Manteyer, G. de, Ed., *Austria's Peace Offer, 1916-1917* (London, 1921)
Massie, Robert K., *Nicholas and Alexandra* (New York, 1967)
Maurois, Andre, *Lyautey* (New York, 1931)
Millis, Walter, *Road to War; America 1914-1917* (Boston, 1935)
Moorehead, Alan, *The Russian Revolution* (New York, 1958)
Pares, Bernard, *The Fall of the Russian Monarchy* (New York, 1939, 1961)
Payne, Robert, *The Life and Death of Lenin* (New York, 1964)
................, *The Rise and Fall of Stalin* (New York, 1965)
Peters, Walter H., *The Life of Benedict XV* (Milwaukee, 1959)
Rauch, Georg von, *A History of Soviet Russia*, rev. ed. (New York, 1959)

Reed, John, *Ten Days That Shook the World* (New York, 1919)

Ritter, Gerhard, *The Sword and the Scepter; the Problem of Militarism in Germany*, Volume III: "The Tragedy of Statesmanship—Bethmann-Hollweg as War Chancellor (1914-1917)" (Coral Gables, Fla., 1972); Volume IV: "The Reign of German Militarism and the Disaster of 1918" (Coral Gables, Fla., 1973)

Rope, Henry E. G., *Benedict XV, the Pope of Peace* (London, 1941)

Salisbury, Harrison E., *Black Night, White Snow: Russia's Revolutions, 1905-1917* (New York, 1978)

Tuchmann, Barbara, *The Guns of August* (New York, 1962)

.............., *The Zimmermann Telgram* (New York, 1958, 1966)

Walsh, William Thomas, *Our Lady of Fatima* (New York, 1947, 1966)

Watt, Richard M., *Dare Call It Treason: the French Army Mutinies, 1917* (New York, 1963)

Wolff, Leon, *In Flanders Fields; the 1917 Campaign* (New York, 1958)

Youssoupoff, Felix, *Rasputin: His Malignant Influence and His Assassination* (London, 1927, 1934)

ALSO AVAILABLE FROM CHRISTENDOM PUBLICATIONS

CALL OF HEAVEN: BRO. GINO, STIGMATIST, by Rev. Robert J. Fox. The biography of a living stigmatist, Bro. Gino Burresi, O.M.V., of San Vittorino, who bears the wounds of Christ and suffers the Passion each Holy Week. Bro. Gino's charisms are presented as signs of God's call to men, making this a rare, inspirational book.

Crossroads, 230 pp., paper, 1982, $3.45

ANNULMENT OR DIVORCE?, by William H. Marshner: a ringing defense of matrimony, attack on current tribunal practice and critique of the proposed revisions of canon law. Treats theological and legal aspects of the problem of easy annulment.

Crossroads, 96 pp., 1978, paper $2.95

REASONS FOR HOPE, ed. J.A. Mirus; authors W.H. Carroll, K.P. Burns, W.H. Marshner. This book by faculty at Christendom College is a complete work of apologetics for the general reader or undergraduate. Ten chapters defend Catholic teaching on God, the Soul, Revelation, Scripture, Christ, Church, Papacy, Dogma and Doctrine.

Christendom College Press, 204 pp., 1978, paper, $5.95

BIOETHICS AND THE LIMITS OF SCIENCE, by Sean O'Reilly, M.D. A Masterful treatment of the ultimate scientific, philosophical and theological issues underlying such current bioethical horrors as abortion and euthanasia. A special appendix on *in vitro* fertilization offers a paradigm for bioethical decisions. Author is post graduate neurobiology research training director at G.W.U. Med. School.

Christendom College Press, 176 pp., 1980, paper $5.95

THE CONSCIOUSNESS OF CHRIST, by Rev. William G. Most. One of the few orthodox scripture scholars of our day proves from Scripture, the Fathers, the Magisterium and speculative theology that Our Lord really did know who He was, even before the Resurrection. Meets an important challenge to Christ's Divinity. A major appendix critiques Biblical form criticism.

Christendom College Press, 232 pp., 1980, paper $5.95

NEWMAN: A BIBLIOGRAPHY OF SECONDARY STUDIES, by John R. Griffin, professor of humanities at the University of Southern Colorado. 2500 entries.

156 pp., 1980, paper, $12.00

THE OXFORD MOVEMENT: A REVISION, by John R. Griffin of U.S.C. Limited edition, reprinted from a series of four articles in *Faith & Reason*. A fresh look at this Anglican movement.

104 pp., 1980, paper $2.50

* * * * * * * *

COMMON FAITH: monthly bulletin of Catholic commentary, edited by J.A. Mirus (Christendom Publications), William H. Marshner (Theology, Christendom College), and Charles E. Rice (Notre Dame Law School). *Common Faith* seeks to reach all Catholics of good will with fast-paced, tart news commentaries featuring family, educational, political and Church problems; careful apologetical reflections on the Faith by the editors; Fr. Robert J. Fox's column offering spiritual counsel; a saint's life in each issue; guest features on vital aspects of Catholicism. Title taken from Romans 1:12.

Price: $10 per year; $25 subscription aids press.

FAITH & REASON: quarterly academic journal edited by J.A. Mirus, Ph.D. and R.V. Young, Ph.D. (N.C. State University). Features 352 pages each year including: articles by Catholic scholars in fields such as theology, philosophy, politics, literature, history and philosophy of science; reviews of significant books of Catholic interest. Assists in developing informed faith.

Price: $15 per year; $25 subscription aids press.

* * * * * * * * *

Please add 90 cents postage for books. Order from:

Christendom Publications
Route 3, Box 87   Front Royal, Virginia 22630